D1472190

THE
NEW
GARCONNE

LAURENCE KING

Published in 2016 by
Laurence King Publishing
361-373 City Road, London,
EC1V 1LR, United Kingdom
T +44 20 7841 6900
F +44 20 7841 6910
enquiries@laurenceking.com
www.laurenceking.com

Reprinted 2016

A catalogue record for this book is available from
the British Library.

ISBN: 978 1 78067 858 0

Design: Masumi Briozzo
Picture researcher: Lucy Maria
Photography on pages 16, 42-47, 54-59, 90-101
© Max Dworkin, www.maxdworkin.com;
pages 66-89, 102 © Elise Toïdé, www.elisetoide.com;
and pages 18-41, 48-53, 60-65 © Kasia Bobula,
www.kasiabobula.com.

Illustrations on pages 142-157 by Masumi Briozzo.

Printed in China

THE
NEW
GARCONNE

How to be a Modern
Gentlewoman

NAVAZ
BATLIWALLA

Laurence King Publishing

Contents

Foreword

Who knew three years ago, that idly 'pinning' pictures of 1920s garconnes and vintage Hermès handbags on a Pinterest board called 'Gentlewoman Style' would result in a book commission? Certainly not me, yet here we are, holding the proof.

The Pinterest board in question is an evolution of my blog, Disneyrollergirl, which I'd started anonymously while working as a fashion editor in 2007. I used the blog to talk about emerging consumer and fashion trends from the point of view of an industry insider, gradually building a loyal following. Over the next few years, as the UK recession took hold, I became increasingly aware of a backlash to our culture of mindless accumulation. Always a quality-conscious shopper, my own fashion choices became even more carefully considered. I only wanted to own the best version of any item, which chimed with the growing appreciation of thoughtful brands such as COS, & Other Stories and Céline, retailers including The Line and La Garçonne, and magazines like *Fantastic Man* and *The Gentlewoman*. This emerging mind-set championed intelligence and lasting style over dumbed-down celebrities and the dreaded 'get the look' culture of fast fashion.

The images collated on my Pinterest board struck a chord with like-minded aesthetes. In their hundreds, they repinned my observations of women who embody a quietly assured, masculine-feminine style. As the idea of 'gentlewoman style' grew in momentum, it occurred to me that the time was right for a book exploring those same gentlewomanly aesthetics and values.

Of course, this was harder than it sounds. My criteria were so specific that it was something of a challenge to find, persuade and schedule the women I really wanted to include. However, tenacity is a wonderful skill to learn! Helped by a patient commissioning editor, generous friends and PR buddies, a certain amount of synchronicity, plus no small amount of LinkedIn stalking, I secured my fourteen favourite 'advocates' to be profiled.

The women featured on these pages reflect the style and sensibility of what I call the New Garconne. They have the same adventurous spirit of their twentieth-century sisters, underscored by grace and sensitivity. In a similar way, some have shunned societal conventions of dress and behaviour. After months of planning, it was a joy to finally transcribe the interviews. What a privilege to relive such honest conversations with these accomplished, creative and collaborative women, who happily dished tales of their challenges and triumphs, both personal and professional. And then guided us through their wardrobe choices to prove that over and above brands and labels, it's the innate personal touches that define style.

To complete these character studies, I enlisted three brilliant photographers who captured the essence of their subjects so intimately. Shooting in their homes and creative studios, in the interest of authenticity we deliberately kept things low-key, free of stylists, assistants, flower arrangers and tidy-uppers. Sheer nosiness aside, I think we can learn a lot by the things a person chooses to surround themselves with.

In our age of downloadable books and photo-sharing apps, the idea of ownership is a funny thing. There's a belief that possessions are somehow shallow but I disagree; we can't help attaching an emotional value to things that represent a moment in time or a personal landmark. As such, the tableaux of sartorial signatures, favourite keepsakes, and well-thumbed books tell their own intriguing stories.

I was also interested in decoding the style signifiers that kept cropping up. Exactly what is it that makes something an enduring classic? And then how do you make it your own? Do you put it away for a while, to be rediscovered and reconfigured later? We've been accustomed to seeing street-style photography of overstyled fashionistas, but the images that resonate the most are of the casual styling gestures that a woman gives to an outfit. Whether that's a haircut, the turn up of a sleeve or a sweater thrown over the shoulders, I think it comes down to having an unapologetic ownership of our style. In the end, it's all about the commitment to being comfortable in our skin, and subsequently, the clothes we're in.

The fearless garconnes of old inform the creative sensibility of today's discerning, cultured, entrepreneurial woman. This introduction explores the provenance and pioneers of a style and attitude that define the New Garconne.

The Heritage

CHAPTER 1

How do we define a gentlewoman today? The word itself is an interesting one, so quaint in one way, yet so thoroughly contemporary in another. As it's not such a commonly used word (other than in the title of the influential magazine, *The Gentlewoman*), I've infused it with my own meaning, which takes a pinch of inspiration from its male equivalent, while adding plenty more spirit, style and individuality.

Let's rewind. The first use of the word gentlewoman emerged around the thirteenth century, and was defined as a woman of noble birth or good social standing. Right for the times, but not so relevant now. But, throughout the twentieth and twenty-first centuries we can note shining examples of women who have stood out for a different kind of nobility; for their daring, innovation, intelligence, independence, creativity and winning sense of style. I'm thinking of the suffragettes and garconnes, Gabrielle 'Coco' Chanel among them, who liberated ladies from constraining corsets and gave them the ease of trousers and oversized knits; and Jeanne Toussaint, the dynamic jewellery director of Cartier, known for her ways with a cocktail pyjama and credited with reinventing jewellery for the twentieth century. Marlene Dietrich and Katharine Hepburn were the garconnes of the silver screen who stood out because they bucked the conventional 'cheesecake' pin-up trend of the time, and looked devastatingly cool with it.

Meanwhile, the worlds of architecture, interior and industrial design have bestowed upon us many brilliant visionaries whose unwavering dedication to improving our surroundings has transformed the way we live. From pioneer of modernity Charlotte Perriand (whose practical room-dividing screens are now part of everyday living) to Andrée Putman, famous for her handsome store interiors and striking looks, we have a debt to pay to these industrious doyennes of design and aesthetics.

For me, the essence of the New Garconne lies in a certain duality. A harmonious yin–yang of masculine and feminine influences; the

Clockwise from above:
Hollywood star Katharine
Hepburn's handsome style was at
odds with the glamorous pin-ups
of the 1940s and 1950s; Jeanne
Toussaint, Cartier's adventurous
creative director of jewellery
from 1933 until 1970; actress
Marlene Dietrich's penchant for
masculine tailoring has influenced
generations of women.

Previous page: Fashion designer
Gabrielle 'Coco' Chanel, whose
interpretations of practical fishing
jerseys and menswear staples
reflected the emancipation of
early twentieth-century women.

Clockwise from right:
Architect and furniture designer
Charlotte Perriand's love of the
outdoors informed her utilitarian
approach to modernist design;
Lee Miller (on the left, with friend
Tanja Ramm); Bianca Jagger's
fearless personal style is
matched by her commitment to
humanitarian and environmental
campaigning work.

highbrow complemented by the humble. Today's informed aesthete appreciates the finer things that life has to offer, but has an equal appreciation of the imperfect and utilitarian. Artist Polly Morgan hankers after Céline trousers but is equally attached to her late father's inexpensive old wristwatch. Perfumer Lyn Harris readily spends on handmade Astier de Villatte ceramics, but totes a cloth bag day to day. Old and new are the most complementary of bedfellows, falling naturally together, whether an antique Chinese vase on a Marc Newson sideboard, or a Dinh Van necklace accessorizing a flea-market sweater.

The most memorable of gentlewomen of the past had a consistent look that married masculine style influences with feminine wit and whimsy. In many cases this came down to circumstances and practical considerations. The army trousers, nonchalantly worn by 1940s Vogue-model-turned-war-correspondent, Lee Miller, for example, were adopted out of necessity, and that same wartime austerity spurred a waste-not-want-not mentality that, for many, has stuck. Practical needs aside, there's a soft sensuality beloved of gentlewomen that should not be dismissed. Hence, in the 1960s, Yves Saint Laurent's muse Betty Catroux's mannish tuxedos were teamed with the finest of silk blouses, and the on-stage uniform of contemporary performers such as Janelle Monáe and Sophie Auster is similarly rooted in a velvet or satin-lapelled trouser suit. Sensuality is the key to the ongoing success of brands such as Margaret Howell and Egg, whose clothes at first sight may seem Amish-like in their asexuality, yet next to the skin feel utterly wonderful. And it's the reason why women such as Sofia Coppola repeat-buy their shirts at Charvet; to the naked eye so simple and unprecious, it's their cut, comfort and quality that sets them apart.

The second decade of this millennium has witnessed a turning point for women. Male and female roles are converging at work and in the home, and the digital revolution has irrevocably accelerated our daily lives. These factors, teamed with globalization and, arguably, a greater appreciation of spiritual matters, have led to a tipping point. Enough of the multi-tasking! We'd like a slower pace, a moment to think, a less consumerist lifestyle and a more mindful existence.

The way we live now is edging towards a more sustainable pace in which we aim to buy less, but better. As women of all ages are fêted for their style and achievements, it is the right time to applaud the personal and individual, not just the fashionable. Maybe that's why I feel there's a renewed interest in how things are made, as well as in objects that have a personal sentimental value. Suddenly, the old William Morris plea for things to be both beautiful and useful has never felt more relevant. Those pieces that are fit for purpose and made to endure, while retaining their good looks, are worth every penny. Time, we're realizing, is the ultimate luxury, in ever shorter supply, and we can't afford to waste it; the things that are designed to last have gained a special resonance with our time-crunched lifestyles.

The gentlewomen I have chosen to interview for this book embody all these values and dualities. They are accomplished, independent women who manage businesses, families and creative practices with passion, grace and a desire for high standards of execution. Their taste is specific and they enjoy surrounding themselves with meaningful things that they love. They're at the vanguard of a movement that's caring, careful, collaborative and empowering and they lead by example.

And so they inspire, not just by their attitude and achievements, but in their dedication to the cause. They have cultivated their own form of empowered dressing that helps get the job done – without becoming a job in itself. What I hope you'll take away is the same sense of positive pragmatism, all dressed up in a cherished blazer and strident (but beautiful) shoes, ready to take on the world.

Clockwise from right: Actress Charlotte Rampling embodies the modern garconne spirit with her choice of nonconformist roles; contemporary performer Janelle Monáe adopts the classic tuxedo for stagewear; actress and activist Jane Birkin's elegant but informal style has enduring appeal.

The fourteen women in the following pages embody the thoughtful style and independent spirit of the New Garconne. From London, Paris and New York, these creatives and entrepreneurs share the stories and style secrets that define them.

The Advocates

CHAPTER 2

Bella Freud

London-based fashion designer Bella Freud grew up surrounded by artists and writers. She is renowned for her eloquent, illustrative sweaters, which have a cult following throughout the world. Her 25-year-old business now encompasses ready-to-wear, scented candles and fragrance, and she has consulted and collaborated with like-minded brands including Fred Perry and Christian Louboutin. A true original, Freud's gentle, boyish aesthetic marries a love of tailoring with an equal passion for the charming and playful.

All my interest in style is about identity and consolidating that, in one way or another. I remember when my father [Lucian Freud] was painting, he would dress in these rags and he'd be covered in paint. But every now and then he'd put his suit on and he just exuded this amazing glamour and authority. He had this aura of confidence, even though he never looked entirely conventional. He often didn't wear a tie but he knotted a scarf and he looked really good in these grey flannel suits. That's how I became obsessed with suits.

I don't like to look masculine but I find boyish quite feminine and quite sexy. I find I can produce my best femininity through that channel and so I've always liked boyish clothes.

It's slightly demoralizing to only dress for comfort. But then, being dressed in a way that makes you stuck in self-consciousness is also not good. You can't be yourself if you're thinking constantly about your waistband, or your knickers

showing, or whatever it is you're wearing that's making you feel awkward.

Proportion is the key thing in any garment. With a jumper it's the shape of the arm, where it becomes narrower, and how tight the bicep is. It's the neatness around the shoulders; it makes a slim silhouette but it's not skintight. I want the jumper to be like a great drawing, like you redraw your silhouette and it gives you a good shadow. Also, if there's a word or image on it, where that comes on the body I like to be quite high up so it's connecting to my brain in some way or other. That way, the jumper isn't just a covering up, it's a 'revealing'.

Reading is really important to me. As a teenager, before there was the internet, there were only books and we didn't have a TV, so I read a lot. At school I became interested in words, in what I chose to express myself with and how succinctly I could nail it. Words and the power of language were everything.

I love the feel of books. I love to have a book in my pocket or in my bag. I like the way they look. If I go into a room and see a load of books, I feel excited. I want to see there's something I haven't seen. It's like an unspoken conversation. It's like seeing someone has something that you like and haven't read, or that you like and have. Immediately there's some sort of connection. It's stimulating.

I do enjoy consuming. I don't consume that much and, in fact, for years and years I never bought anything. I definitely don't look and see what the 'new thing' is; I don't really work like that. If I buy something that's a bit crummy, I find it slightly lowering. There's a weird sort of test that happens when I do go shopping. I think, 'Am I really going to *buy* this?'

I don't have a fragrance ritual. But I usually spray it around my hair and neck, so that's what someone gets if they get that close to me; and on my wrists and on my clothes. Putting perfume on is like a micro moment. It's like, OK this is me, this is what you're going to get. It's quite intimate. Without having to strip naked, it's like a tiny drawing-in, like reading the same book. 'Oh, you've read that book? Oh, you're wearing that? Oh yes, I've read that!'

I'm really into black coffee, getting a buzz off that and getting my notebook out.

A new notebook is a real pleasure. It means that I've finished an old notebook so I've filled it up with drawings.

There's always a resistance in putting something down in case it's not right. But drawing – even if I don't know what I'm going to draw – makes things happen, so it's a really important part of making ideas come to life. I love things to do with paper and a pen and a pencil. I don't enjoy the computer very much at all, unless I'm writing.

I like, on a Friday, going down Golborne Road near my studio [in Notting Hill]. There's the local Portuguese and Moroccan market stalls and it's a really good vibe because it hasn't been tarted up. There are a few really good places for coffee, and friendly people, like the local dry-cleaner that sells my charity's Palestine scarves. You'll have interesting conversations walking down Golborne Road; it's a great atmosphere.

I think it's important to have a beginning and end of the day for the studio. Generally, I like people to leave when they're supposed to leave instead of working too long hours. I know that isn't necessarily productive. We're a small team but very close and I like to think that people are happy.

It's funny, ambition is not approved of but I think it's good to be ambitious so I hope I am.

I want the business to stay authentic, I want it to grow and be successful but I don't want to do things for the sake of them. I want there to be a reason behind doing everything and for it to be interesting and seem like a good idea to me. And to do things with the same focus and the same dedication, as if it was the only thing I was doing.

I recently opened my first shop and I want it to mean everything, for when you go in there to feel like you have some kind of feeling of connection, not just a consumer experience. That's my big challenge, how do I make it work?

I have to organize my life so that there are as many ideas coming in as going out. And as much drawing on notebooks, because that will make all that happen, rather than just rushing and doing things for the sake of them. That requires delegation, having amazing people around me who I feel I admire and I trust, who bring me things and … we get on well. That's absolutely crucial. I couldn't work with someone I didn't like. It's about valuing people and the experience of working and being rigorous at the same time.

Lyn Harris

As a rebellious Yorkshire youth with a talent for fragrance, Lyn Harris took herself to Paris and found her calling as a perfumer. Success followed, with her luxury fragrance brand, Miller Harris, leading to commissions for heritage clients including Manolo Blahnik, Liberty and LVMH. With a love for all things natural and British, the latest chapter in Harris's story is Perfumer H, a bespoke atelier that puts the feel-good factor into fragrance and celebrates the importance of creative collaboration.

I was always secretly ambitious. My father's an entrepreneur, so from an early age I watched him build a very successful business in architecture and that deeply inspired me.

I wasn't academic but I loved fashion and I was really into scent. My parents had a good friend who owned a beautiful perfume shop in Halifax, so I went to work there. I was dreaming and reading these amazing books on Chanel, Patou, the House of Guerlain, and thinking, 'Oh, why can't I do something like this?'

I moved to London to stay with my sister and worked with Aromatherapy Associates for a year. Out of the blue, I read about a woman in Paris who had recently opened a fragrance school, so I just took myself to see her. Whatever I had, I knew I had a talent. And I was driven, but through intuition and passion. My parents were big fragrance people; my mum had the Santa Maria Novella fragrances and I grew up in a nice house with a garden where we grew beautiful flowers.

At school, I was the one who would set a trend, because I was a bit of a rebel. I've always been an individual; I've never followed. I wasn't scared of doing anything.

I've always dressed the same; it's kind of boyish. I love a good pair of jeans. I'm one of those people, I'll obsess about getting the best pair of jeans, and I think it's only now I feel like, 'God, I've been through all that, tried every pair of jeans, and I'm back to A.P.C.' I know that they're the best because I've tried them all!

My design taste is eclectic, but I suppose I'm a bit of a modernist. I love living in an open-plan apartment because I like the European openness. But stick me in the countryside and I'll be in a cottage.

I'm really into nature and the seasons. I love to collect things from my walks; I drive everyone crazy with my pieces of moss! When I'm walking, I'm always working. I'll have ideas just sitting here, but they actually start working when I'm close to nature – always when I'm walking or in the garden – because I'm surrounded by beauty and nature and I'm thinking about these different fragrance notes and things, and it just all comes into place.

My grandparents were a big influence. My grandfather was a carpenter and my grandmother was cooking all the time. That kind of sensuality woke me up and has stayed with me. When I'm creating, I go back to those days, with the smells and the smoke. It's all about memory and how that memory develops with time. It accumulates and you come up with this amazing fragrance with all these different experiences.

Everything's so artificially scented these days but, used positively, scent can really enhance our lives. Scenting the home should be all about using beautiful ingredients in your candles.

Writing in a notebook feels real. I've done this since I was in Paris, as I'm always writing formulas and ideas. I like Clairefontaine notebooks and I keep them all.

I've always spent quite a bit on skincare and I like massaging my face in the evening. I like doing all that. Getting ready in the morning? No, I don't think about it, I just want to be out the door.

I don't wear fragrance during the day because it distracts me from my work, so I'll wear it when I go out. I really love it that, when I'm greeting someone, they can smell it and I can smell it as well. I like to cocoon myself. I also like the back of the ears, that's quite nice, especially when you've got long hair.

I don't like to be too dressed up. I've always got to have some kind of rebellious element. I'll wear an army jacket to a meeting with my bank, but it's only in the last few years that I'd feel comfortable doing that. This wisdom has kicked in. Putting on a power blazer to go to a meeting is so not me.

I wear Solange Azagury-Partridge jewellery. She's got a real talent in the way she puts stones together. My rings are from her; they're good for adding a feminine touch.

My husband's family is from Brittany, so I will disappear for two hours and go to these funny little fishing shops and stock up on Breton stripes and nautical blazers. I've got some old ones that are amazing, and they're affordable too.

My brand is about authenticity, integrity in what you produce, and not compromising. I want to give a beautiful experience to everybody who comes in the door, whether it's an experience into how a perfumer works, or it's the beauty of the handblown glass with beautiful smells inside. I don't just want to be another thing for wealthy people to buy.

I have a lot of Astier de Villatte ceramics from France. You can feel the integrity of their work, it's very special and it just adds something when you're eating or just having tea.

I love tea, the ritual of it and the taste - especially Postcard Teas. It's part of my creativity. There's a lot of frustration in what I do - 'Oh god, I haven't got it, that smell, it's nearly there.' So then I'll make a cup of tea. I'm a bit northern like that; whenever there's a disappointment it's like your mum saying, 'Come on then, let's have a cup of tea!'

How I am in life is how I am in business. I'm very giving and probably too trusting, but I like being like that. I never stop believing in people, I'm always positive and there's always a solution.

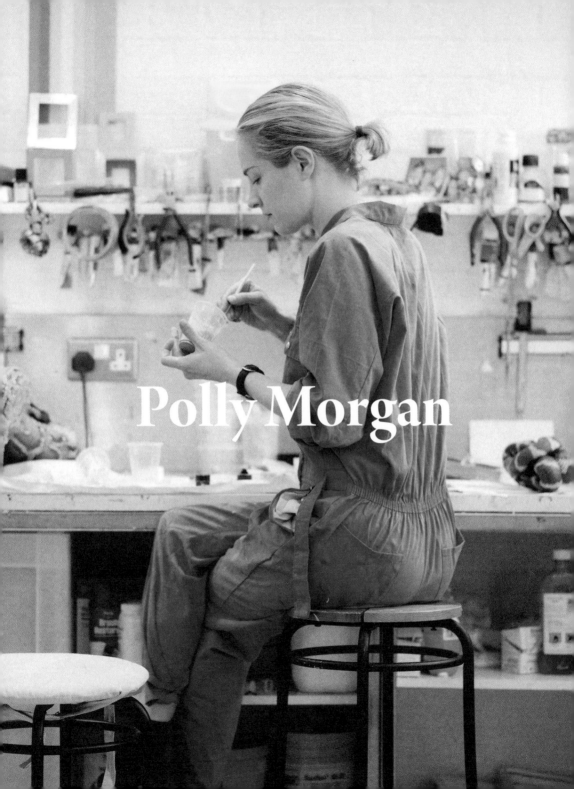

Polly Morgan

Polly Morgan arrived in the contemporary art world having moved to London from Oxfordshire to study English literature. She has established herself as a sculptor who uses taxidermy as her medium in a bold, modern way, learning the art of taxidermy herself simply because she couldn't find a piece she liked. She is recognizable by her handsome, pared-back style. A fixture on the East London art scene, she entertains artist friends in the flat above her Hackney Wick studio.

I was quite naive when I started out. I had a slight 'anything goes' approach. The more art that I see and learn about, the more self-critical I am as an artist. If anything, even though I think I'm making better work now than I ever have before, I'm less happy with it than I was, because I still feel I've got a long way to go and there's a lot of room for improvement.

If you make your work with money in mind you're not going to be making good work because what you're trying to do is get into the head of a collector and decide what they want. That's not really art, that's just being a salesperson.

I equate inactivity with failure so, in order to stave off feelings of self-doubt, I'm always busy. I'm always doing something and, if I'm not working, I'll go running or, if I'm not running, I'll cook. I need to see the fruits of my labour all the time. I need to feel that I've done something, and cooking's good for that. It serves a purpose as well.

Everything in my studio is functional. There are no decorative objects, apart from art on the walls. I hate ornamentation; I just find it clutters my space or my mind. The worst presents I can be given are ornaments - or a decorative box. I love tools though. I like collecting them for my studio; anything that makes my life easy.

All the works of art I have mean something. Most are gifts from friends, so I never want to get rid of them. I bought the Celia Hempton painting (opposite, top left) when my dad died. We sold the house and had a bit of money, so I really wanted to buy something I'd keep forever.

Art fairs are a bit of an odd environment. The Venice Biennale can be fun if you're involved in some way. Venice is amazing because it's such an extraordinary-looking place, and you travel by boat so it's a thrilling place to be. Berlin's good if you want to go and see art and have a really chilled-out time.

I would collect art if I had more money. If money were no object I'd collect Blinky Palermo, Agnes Martin and Boo Saville, who does minimal, colour-field paintings that are lovely. I love Donald Judd sculptures too. Weirdly, the work that I love is different to the work that I make.

If things have a function, and they make my life easier, then I'm definitely 'pro' technology. I photograph all my own work and, over the years, I've taught myself Photoshop and now I can edit photos quite well. I've never really got into social media but I thought I'd try Instagram. It's visual and I'm an artist so it makes perfect sense for me. A lot of people who follow me like to see the work in progress. Unless you know taxidermy, quite often the pictures of the things I'm working on are just unidentifiable. They're really weird things you've never seen before, like a skin inside out, sort of facing its own skull.

I've always had a strong sense of my own taste. I never wanted to fit in or to be part of a group. I'm not always the most confident person but I've always had the confidence to stand behind my choices, even if they've been monstrous decisions with clothes, or furniture, or my art.

I like to dress like an Italian businessman. I wear very loose-fitting masculine clothes and, because of the work I do and being in overalls a lot of the time, I like going out looking like I'm a businesswoman. Or businessman! I like the cut of men's clothes; I'm not a fan of the nipped-in waist.

I wear a lot of Acne Studios clothes, especially their trousers and shirts and I've got a really nice big overcoat. What I like about them is they don't cut womenswear with that sucky-in waist thing; they always have things straight cut and they have good cashmeres and wools and cottons. I also love Céline, but I can't usually afford that so I go to Bicester Village [an outlet shopping centre] occasionally and buy it there.

I'm not a big jewellery person but I like a gold chain and just to stick things on it sometimes. A friend gave me my favourite pendants. One is a Rich Tea biscuit with a bite out of it that Gavin Turk did. And there's a screw pendant I like because it's a tool.

My beauty routine is ridiculously simple and, as I grow older, I realize it's more important. I've discovered that things like a good haircut and well-applied make-up make a big difference. I think if your eyebrows look good, you don't even need make-up. I'm extremely low maintenance, but I'm trying to get better at taking time to do that.

I'd rather buy an expensive coat that I'd then wear for years, or a cashmere jumper, than lots of cheap ones. I think that's a much more sensible way of going about things anyway, because it's better quality. And all that throwaway stuff is just horrible; I hate waste.

If I'm dressing up, I wear Givenchy heels. They're very plain, strappy sandals and they're very expensive so I buy them in the sale on Net-a-Porter. I like minimal, simple heels – nothing too crazy.

I go running with my dogs in the morning before work. It's a really good way to start the day; I feel worn out, in a good way. It makes me feel stronger. It's like having a shot of espresso, you feel really buzzy when you come back.

Caroline Issa

As CEO of the Tank Group, Caroline Issa is a master juggler. When not publishing *Tank* magazine and managing its print, digital and consultancy divisions, she is the street-style superstar, with a penchant for masculine tailoring and finely crafted shoes, who also designs her own line for Nordstrom. The London-based former management consultant, of half-Singaporean, half Lebanese-Iranian descent, excels in contradictions. She wears minimal make-up but loves a red lip, and she's a tech whizz with an addiction to paper diaries and novelty Post-its.

Growing up, I spent my summers in Singapore where I had a very glamorous auntie. As I veered into my teens, she would take me on her shopping trips. Even then, the idea of luxury brands was just starting to seep into my brain. Singaporeans love a big logo and a big brand, but she was always so glamorous and beautifully put together.

My family home was always made up of things from the East and Middle East, including beautiful Singaporean antique stuff. My aunt on my dad's side was a contemporary Middle East expert, so we were lucky to have lovely things in the house from very different cultures. But, growing up in Montreal, everything was really new, so we'd have new and old sitting next to each other.

Good design has to speak to you, there has to be something emotional. It has to improve your life, whether that's in an 'absolute beauty' sense or in a functionality sense. I think, when something is well designed, it makes your life simpler, richer and just better.

I gravitate towards trouser suits and shirts. Especially classic suits in great fabrics in an amazing cut. Because then you can add, say, a printed coloured shirt and look like you've made an effort when actually you really haven't! I have an Armani suit, I have a Gucci, I have a Tom Ford and I've started making my own at Nordstrom. The fun thing I've learned from designing the Nordstrom collections is that it's all about the details. How many buttons do you want? How long do you want the jacket? Where does it hit? There are so many details you take for granted when you pick something off the rack. The challenge for me was figuring out the right level of 'classic with a twist', with the right amount of quality.

One of my favourite jewellery brands is Monique Péan. She has a wonderful sustainability model built into her fine jewellery business and she uses incredible materials, so I like to collect her stuff. I love chunky things and I like really fine things; I go between those two extremes.

I would describe my style as a balance between masculine and feminine. I'm not typically very feminine in that I don't love frilly ruffles or chiffon. But I buy a lot of menswear-inspired pieces. Longer pinstripe shirting, oversized sweaters and menswear-inspired shoes like brogues are great.

The more I learn about the fashion business, the more I'm convinced that people need to buy less but buy better. I haven't shopped the high street in a very long time because I'm very conscious of the wastage and the copying. They both go a little bit hand in hand. So I try to buy luxury, originality and craftsmanship when I can, then I know where things are made and sourced. I don't preach it but I try to live my own life that way.

I wear so little make-up that skin is the most important thing, so I spend the most money on my cleansers and moisturizers – although I go between Cetaphil, an American drugstore cleanser, and Susanne Kaufmann, which is expensive but organic and it just really works.

I bulk-buy red lipsticks. I have far too many red lipsticks but I keep going back to the Shu Uemura one, a matte red from the Yazbukey collaboration. It's petal soft and it stays forever.

I'm obsessed with a cosmetics store in Paris called Buly 1803 and I love the candle shop, Cire Trudon, run by the same guy. I love it when retail tells an amazing story, with great packaging, and everything fits together to create a beautiful world.

When people can write well it's such a brilliant gift. I wish I could photograph, I wish I could sew, I wish I could craft. If I could bedazzle, I'd bedazzle everything! But when it comes to my own creative outlet, I love to read fiction. Books get me excited and get my imagination soaring.

I like to use social media as a fun communication, as a marketing platform and to share discoveries. But you don't want technology to intrude in your life; you want technology to help your life.

I'm becoming a master multi-tasker. I'm juggling a number of different things but I've always loved that. I tend to have quite a rigid schedule, which is annoying because it means spontaneity is very rare. Professionally, I'm a fantastic multi-tasker. Personally? I don't have kids. I don't know how people with kids and jobs do everything.

My desk is organized chaos. There are four different diaries, even though I should just be using one, and lots of Post-it notes. There are a lot of personal, meaningful things next to efficient to-do lists, next to my pile of papers that I need to go through. We have a bookshop and a flower shop for us, just to surround ourselves with beautiful and interesting things, which is really nice. We try to make this a place where people aren't, 'Ugh, I have to go to the office.'

I feel like I'm friendly and approachable, but I do expect a lot. This is a tough, very competitive business. We're a small team and everyone has to be brilliant at what they do, so I expect and desire excellence from my team. I have high expectations but I think everybody who works in a creative place should want to put out the most amazing thing that they can.

A gentlewoman has kindness and some traditional values, like loyalty and gentleness and respect. And, at the same time, she's a woman who's powerful and fearless and up for many adventures.

Kris Kim

A childhood magazine fixation led Korean-born New Yorker Kris Kim to careers in fashion design and PR. But things crystallized when she founded La Garçonne, a retail destination that threads all her interests and know-how together. A typography and modernism fiend, her store, e-shop and in-house label La Garçonne Moderne embody the singular aesthetic that attracts her loyal customers. And, a similar focus permeates her family's home, a meditative haven of Scandi design and Noguchi lamps in the heart of Tribeca.

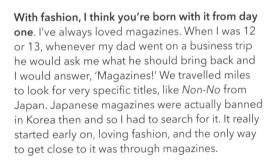

With fashion, I think you're born with it from day one. I've always loved magazines. When I was 12 or 13, whenever my dad went on a business trip he would ask me what he should bring back and I would answer, 'Magazines!' We travelled miles to look for very specific titles, like *Non-No* from Japan. Japanese magazines were actually banned in Korea then and so I had to search for it. It really started early on, loving fashion, and the only way to get close to it was through magazines.

I studied fashion design and when I graduated I worked in New York as a colourist, spending a lot of time on a light-box making sure colours matched. I still have a deep love for construction and everything's a colour story to me. I also worked for magazines and worked in PR for ten years, including working for Prada in Korea, then Katayone Adeli, Hogan and Hermès in New York.

The PR end of fashion taught me to understand the business and how important the imagery and marketing are – the packaging, the authenticity of it all. It turned out to be a good school for what I'm doing now. What I've come to realize is that if you're creating something, then you believe in it. Everything has to be from the core; you have to understand what your point of view is to do anything. It's hard to fake it.

As a little girl, I would sketch out these looks or ideas for everything, from a pillow to dresses. I had no idea what that meant in real life, but they were hints that that's what I was interested in. Then, after doing public relations for a long time, I realized I have this love for all these things and I knew somehow that these objects made sense in an environment. That environment, where I could be creative, meant having my own store. At the time I'd had my first child and there were a lot of things up in the air. I thought, 'Oh, I can do this on my own as a side project and do this thing called "online".'

With La Garçonne, it's not just about having a brand for the sake of having a brand. I think we truly understand who comes to us, who seeks us out – their lives, their wardrobes, their everyday routine. There's an emotional connection there. In the end, we're all the same people: we're looking for our friends – that shared philosophy where things have to be meaningful.

My personal goal is to define the ten or so pieces that I can make into my own uniform. Because of the nature of my job, I'm exposed to so much and I think it's about picking all the noise away a little bit. The older you get, the more you tend to narrow it down, and I'm excited about narrowing down.

Lately I've been wearing a lot of the label I design called Moderne. About three years ago I designed a line of basic sweaters, because it was so hard to find a nice crew neck and V-neck in the colours that I like. A season later we added pants, a jacket, and it went from there. It was inspired by the artist in all of us, hence the 'artist jacket' or the 'writer pant'. It represents this modern woman, who isn't afraid to be feminine but also has a mannish spirit.

I like dainty jewellery and I love watches. I have a couple of Hermès watches. They're something that I always go back to. They're quietly beautiful and elegant, and an absolute classic.

I was always envious of those women who could wear red lipstick but I gravitated more towards the cleaner, no make-up look: a little bit of mascara, a little bit of gloss. That's always been an important ingredient for La Garçonne too, to

capture this idea of the natural woman who, it's not as if she doesn't have any make-up on, but just not too much of it. And the hair as well. It's natural and effortless but that doesn't mean that's it's messy – just kept a little undone. I think there's a great beauty to that.

On my desk I have a Fuji camera, a Leica and an agenda, a real agenda that you write on. I'm not much of a planner but I have been trying to make an effort to go back to how it was done before. I think it's a good thing and I'm trying to set an example and teach my kids that that's important. And then I have a bunch of books, favourite magazines and little plants everywhere.

I can't get enough of the Noguchi lamp – it's a wonderful object. We have three in the office, two in the store and three at home.

My favourite place to visit is Seoul, because of the friends and family I have there. So much is happening there right now, it's a really exciting city. They're so passionate about fashion and they always have a lot of fun.

Right now, it's a good time to be an individual and do what you want to do. Where the point of inspiration is, is almost not relevant. All of those references, whether it's 1980s or 1990s, or even more recent, it's all relevant at the same time. I feel like we've ridden those times; it's not just one trend or just one thing happening.

Donna Wallace

As the accessories editor of *Elle* magazine, Londoner Donna Wallace's taste informs the shopping choices of thousands. With access to endless fashion riches, her exacting editor's eye distils the sea of seasonal offerings into the most enduring buys on the high street. Balancing the breakneck pace of fashion with modern media has become a game in which a playful approach to time comes in handy. And, whether it's affordable fashion or luxury investment, Wallace's lifelong appreciation for quality and design is the common denominator.

As a child, I used to love watching my grandmother get ready for church. It was a Pentecostal church, so always very energetic and vibrant and 'happy clappy'. There was a certain formality and that's when I first became aware of needing to be appropriately dressed, what goes with what and how to put outfits together.

Working with [former *Elle* fashion director] Iain R. Webb early in my career informed my look. He was very up for experimental dressing, boyish dressing. I loved what he was wearing and, as a junior, I was absorbing everything around me. When I think about the components in my day-to-day dress – the jeans, the tailoring – it's very much how he dresses.

Women's fashion is treated as though you're not going to want to keep it, although brands are now beginning to understand that a woman doesn't want to wear something for five minutes and then throw it away.

It's easier to find masculine cuts in womenswear offerings now. Céline is a given, everything is brilliantly executed. I also love Acne Studios, Church's shoes and J.W. Anderson.

A good coat is the hardest thing for the high street to do well, even though, workwise, that's where my head is a lot of the time. & Other Stories make very good coats. I want to wear mine all the time.

I have always preferred to get the best version of the thing I want rather than buy a quick fix. Even if it's a high-street piece, it will still be the best version of the high-street piece that I will buy.

Accessories allow me to get into the little details of something and geek out a bit. I find the craftsmanship, the expertise and the mechanics of watches really interesting and the geek in me always wants to know more. I like the stealth nature of an Hermès Médor or the Jaeger-LeCoultre Reverso; I like how you can't tell that it's a watch. I'm also blown away by the Dior watches, they have colours that you wouldn't see on another watch. Where else would you see a maroon and blue watch? For a modern watch, it's the kind of watch I'll still love in 20 years.

Sometimes, I turn time into a game where I've got X amount of hours to do Y. If I have a particularly busy day when some serious stuff needs to happen, then I'll grab an inexpensive watch from the *Elle* fashion cupboard and be like, 'Right, I'm getting related to the time', and become more playful with the day. You could be stressed about it, or you could dance in it.

I've become a morning person. It means I can chill out a bit, be calm, claw back parts of the day that belong only to me. That's a big change to me. I had this epiphany: 'Maybe I'm supposed to be up at this time!' If I don't feel broken by nine or ten AM, then maybe it's working.

I play big when there's something I need to make happen in a work capacity, but then, when there's something *I* need to happen, I don't always play it in the same way. The trick is to apply that same skill and mental muscle to anything else that you want for yourself. A lot of times I forget that, but it's really important.

When I put outfits together, I'm often thinking how to soften it. When you have short hair you have to consider that much more, because there's no ponytail that's going to be flipping around. It makes you consider what's going to offset this. The colour? The heel? But then, sometimes, it depends on my frame of mind. Some days I can roll with the punches and other days it needs to be offset with an element of softness.

Even if I'm in love with a shoe, if I can't walk in it, I'm just not going to do it. It's about being able to get where I'm going, even if I'm wearing a heel. The lucite heels on my Dior boots do it for me, combined with the weirdness of the fabric and the glossiness. It's so appealing; it adds something – a weird full stop. And they're comfortable.

I try not to have a high-maintenance beauty routine. I like to use a facial oil by Antipodes and I try to keep things as low key and mindful of ingredients as possible; so, natural but effective. There are lots of brands now that are science-based but from nature. That's why I like facial oils; they seem to work for me.

I always want to do something really well. It bothers me if I don't do it well, it doesn't sit easy with me. I like to be able to do things properly and thoroughly.

The place I love to escape to is the conservatory at the Barbican [performing arts centre]. The feeling you get in there is extraordinary, it's so green and lush, it's like being in a rainforest or jungle. It's like the Hanging Gardens of Babylon but in a building, all cascading down through the balconies and concrete.

Jill Nicholls

A sculptor turned set designer and interior decorator, New York-based Brit Jill Nicholls grew up around beautiful forms. From her London post-punk youth spent thrifting in Camden, to creating shoot sets for *Vogue*, an eye for the unexpected informs her style. Away from the frenzy of fashion, she finds solace in her study, surrounded by her children's art.

I grew up in London where my dad was a Queen's Counsel and my mum stayed at home. My brothers were sent to private school, while we girls went to the local school, because my parents were of a mind that the boys were the breadwinners and we would be the wives and mothers. It was a contentious subject when we were growing up but, in retrospect, I think we were lucky. We had the freedom to be what we wanted, while my brothers had the pressure to do something sensible.

I was smart at school but not interested. I rebelled and came out with one O Level in English Literature. I never passed art but I ended up with a scholarship to do a master's in sculpture at Syracuse University so, at 23, I went to America on my own. Then I was going to go and work for a sculptor in New Mexico but that fell through so I moved to New York City. I got a job doing Barneys' windows with Simon Doonan, which I did freelance, really as a way to make money.

I found a studio for about $200 a month and I stayed at people's houses for six months. When I arrived in New York, I lost interest in sculpture for a while but then I got a job working for the artist Richard Prince for three years. I loved it; he was a great boss. I worked in my studio and started making all these vanity units. They were related to the ritual of doing your hair and make-up because I was interested in rituals and performance.

I got into set design quite late, at the age of 34, by working for a friend who was doing commercials and movies. One day, he suggested I come and be a shopper for a fashion shoot he was doing and I really enjoyed it. I decided, 'I want to do this'; it was working with furniture, fabrics and all the things I understand.

Set design made sense because it's storytelling. I was brought up among beautiful paintings, furniture, antiques and objects, and that's the same sort of world. Although my parents were traditional, my mum has quite a twisted eye. The objects she buys are everywhere. Not on top of each other, but carefully displayed.

Some of the best work I've done has been with Lucinda Chambers for British *Vogue*. I love those jobs because she lets you do your thing. But I've realized there's a creative ceiling in set design, so now I'm also doing interior decorating. That's all about who the clients are, who I think them to be and what I think they will love. There are so many things you have to take into consideration, it can be overwhelming but I've never really been someone who gets put off by fear.

It's important always to be a bit nervous because, in my experience, you don't know everything, you're always still learning.

My study is calm, simple and really small, which is how I want it. It helps me concentrate. It has an L-shaped desk and on it are a few specific objects. There's my frosted-glass mushroom lamp, some paperweights with little flowers in them and a Chinese lacquered plate. And then there's a wall full of my kids' drawings.

My favourite object is my orange chair, which is contemporary Danish. It's upholstered in orange silk velvet with these beautifully formed arms; it's elegant but it's not practical. For me, it's really about the beauty, the story and an emotion.

I've always loved clothes. As soon as I had my own job, at 15, I went to Camden Market all the time. I had bright pink stirrup trousers and would wear tails to parties. These days I love Dries Van Noten but I get it from Century 21, which requires you to look very carefully. But I don't need to pay full price and I can't afford to!

There's a great flea market in Fort Greene every Saturday in the summer and in the winter it's in Crown Heights. It sells good food, jewellery and clothes and has a stall selling beautiful French fishermen's sweaters and dress shirts.

I love jewellery but I don't wear a lot of it. I have six pairs of Ted Muehling earrings. I have a lot of earrings because my mum has an incredible jewellery collection; it's very eclectic and it's all real.

Lots of profound things have happened in the last few years to change my outlook. The most important things are just to be really present with everything that's in front of you and appreciate what you have. I'm passionate about work but it doesn't dictate my self-worth.

The best thing is when I'm in my study, my kids are at school and my husband's playing the piano. I'm working, I'm in an amazing creative zone and it's the most peaceful, content and pure feeling.

Chloe Lonsdale

Chloe Lonsdale grew up absorbing the influences of her parents' jeans business, Jean Machine. In 2006, she launched her own denim line, marrying her love of authentic denim with a passion for boyish shirting and a good slouchy sweater. As Chief Creative Officer (CCO) of M.i.H. Jeans, with husband Johan as CEO, she relishes weekend time with the kids in her Sussex home or escaping to the outdoor calm of Big Sur, California.

I went to a school with no uniform so every day was a bit of a fashion show. At 13 or 14 I discovered all my dad's jeans. Until then I hadn't registered how my dad's business permeated through how he represented himself, how he dressed and his trunks in the attic full of jeans. So, jeans became my thing very early on. I could wear them every day to school and cut off the hems and dye them and do what I wanted.

A good pair of jeans is a combination of fit, feel and fabrication but ultimately it's how they make you feel when you pull them on. Denim does need to be quite robust and just *that* shade of blue. It has to be indigo; you're never going to find me in a pair of black jeans!

If I put on an oversized shirt, I instantly roll the sleeves up. It allows a slender part of your body to show, which I think is the most feminine thing. I love nothing more than wearing one of my husband's sweaters with a slim pair of jeans and some great shoes to balance it out. If you wear something oversized, you balance it with a part of your body on show, or you have a slimmer silhouette on the bottom or top.

It would be nice to own a grown-up watch at some point. I love to wear one piece of jewellery or one watch, and it's the one thing I don't have. I like the Hermès Double Tour strap watches; the combination of the leather and the metal together is lovely. And they're quite slim, which is really nice on my wrist.

I don't think good skin is about layering products and eye cream. Having a healthy lifestyle, wearing sunscreen, staying super-hydrated and drinking lots of water – those are the things that contribute to glowing skin, as well as genes. I'm a bit sceptical about the huge skincare market out there. There are great products, but I don't think you need tons of them.

I love to have the feeling of water on my face to clean it. Everything in my life needs to be touched with water. I love to swim, all my clothes have to be washed; the thought of dry-cleaning just freaks me out!

I probably wear perfume once every couple of weeks. I prefer to smell clean. I'm always so afraid of having that overpowering strong scent that I prefer to be in a scented environment. So I love filling the house with flowers and, as an alternative, always a scented candle from Diptyque or Bella Freud.

I don't shun consumerism. I'm seduced by design and by brands sometimes, but I edit quite carefully what I want and what I feel is important. When I make a purchase it's a very thought-out thing. I'd never go out and get lots of things in one go. Whether it's my home or a wardrobe, it's slowly building and adding to it over time so it becomes part of you.

Good design has to look good and work well. I'm hugely into aesthetics, but if it's useless and doesn't have a function then it doesn't have any worth to me. I have to have that balance between practicality and being visually appealing.

Chairs are the kind of thing that embodies great design. I love Eames chairs; they're so basic and ergonomic. The curve and the juxtaposition of materials, from the ash leg to the fibreglass base, look beautiful, yet they're also functional.

There is always a pen and a notebook in my bag. I'm part of a generation that likes to write things down and I think it will stay with me. Photos, pictures and books – they're things of life. I have never considered stripping back those things.

My desk at work has a stack of books and a stack of spreadsheets. I go between meetings with spreadsheets and projects, inspiration books and boards. So there's always quite a balance on my desk between creative and business paraphernalia. I have a huge mood board behind my desk so I'm always changing the images. There's also a stack of vintage garments. I try to

go to Portobello Market every few weeks and build up a collection at work. I always have a vase of flowers on my desk.

Sometimes people over-think the perfect work-life balance. If you're trying to grow a business, or you're dedicated to a job or your career, and you have kids, they're going to merge. As long as you're self-aware enough to manage it, if you have kids and a career, you put them to bed and you work in the evening and it's what you've decided to do.

Early on in my business, I just kind of winged it, but, however you get there, it's tremendously hard work. I would recommend anyone else starting a business today to plan it more. I learned a lot by doing it the first few years by myself, but I hadn't worked in the industry long enough. So, I'd recommend anyone to make sure they research all areas of the business. When you're 25 and you've worked for two years in a company, that's not enough to really know how things work.

Swimming and being outside are two really important things for me. I love travel and the travelling I get to do for work is a treat. It gives me a wonderful perspective because I'm a mum, so it gives me a real opportunity to explore. I love California, especially Big Sur. It's a very, very special place. The scenery is incredible. Wherever I can see the sea, I'm happy.

Sophie Hersan

Sophie Hersan is the supply quality director of Vestiaire Collective and an excellent advertisement for the luxury consignment marketplace she co-founded in 2009. With her meticulous eye and natural appreciation for genuine style, she has helped shape the way we consume fashion in a more considered, eco-aware way. Off-duty, this nature-loving homebody is happiest relaxing in the Ibizan hills or in her Paris garden, surrounded by lemon trees, herb bushes and her beloved cats, Romeo and Lily.

My first idea of 'taste' came from my mother, but it was more an 'attitude' with her clothes. I was also inspired by what I saw in the magazines: what a woman could wear and a freedom that I could feel.

I grew up in a traditional medical family in a little town in Champagne, in France. My parents let me go to Paris when I was 17. I should have gone into economics but it wasn't my destiny.

After attending fashion school I became a stylist and studio director for 15 years. I was inspired by very feminine, sexy and modern women, as long as it didn't turn out to be vulgar. I worked with Eric Sartori who was the first assistant of Azzedine Alaïa. As studio director, I learned how to be the interface between the creativity and the commercial, and to help the designer to realize what he has in his head.

I don't believe in fate but in moments. I met Vestiaire Collective co-founder Sébastien Fabre, who had a strong conviction of the need for a new marketplace, dedicated to fashion but with a focus on inspiration, editorial and community, as well as recycling.

It's important for us to respect the luxury brands' universe. That's why we make the selection and that's why we have the quality control. It's why, today, we have lots of collaborations with the brands and good relationships. We help each other.

I value rings from my grandmother, watches from my mother, lots of things that my family gave me. An emotional attachment is important to me. To wear something old to me is modern. It's emotional because it's from my family, but also because of the story that comes with a piece that is 60 years old.

I wear a watch to tell the time. During the holidays, I don't wear watches because I don't need to track the time. I love the watch as an object, though, too. I don't have many watches but all are vintage; there's a Cartier one, a Rolex one, a gold one.

I love denim; I wear it in any circumstances. I like A.P.C. jeans, but only the pre-worn ones that you can buy at the boutique. And I never wash them with water; I always dry-clean my jeans.

I always wear the same things. I need to be well dressed but comfortable, so I wear shirts, especially Céline, poplin shirts or denim shirts. I wear my shirts and jackets with the sleeves pushed up, even if I'm dressing someone else. I do it automatically, maybe because of the need to feel comfortable and not restricted.

I like to mix vintage pieces and more modern objects. It's a big mix but I love that because objects need to tell a story. Fashion books tell me stories, more than novels. I like design books, because you can open, close and read them over and over again.

More and more I prefer natural beauty products. I like Aēsop, Buly 1803 and citrus fragrances from Santa Maria Novella. I like things that look old, so I love the Buly 1803 concept. The boutique looks so old-fashioned, the lotions smell great, it's natural and I love the packaging.

I love different smells in the house so I always have flowers, spices, herbs and fragrances around me. I like contrasts, so in the living room there is lots of wood to create a warm atmosphere but mixed with very brutal materials.

Dominique Cathelin, the landscape gardener of the concept store Merci [in Paris], designed my garden. I wanted something natural and poetic, something that I can see growing, so I have Mediterranean trees, lots of roses, herbs and olives.

My simple pleasures are my two cats, Romeo and Lily, and morning walks in the garden, especially during spring. I love to watch nature live and change.

I work a lot but the other part of my life needs to be simpler, more authentic and always keeping in mind absolutely where I came from. I often go to Ibiza. Sometimes you discover somewhere in your life that matches you, that feels like home. I read once that the island makes people crazy, but I'm sure I'm not crazy when I go there! But I do feel something.

I love going to the Café de Flore in Paris. So many writers and artists went there and I also remember having lunches with Chloé founder, Gaby Aghion. I respected her a lot. She was a fantastic, passionate and fascinating modern woman who would tell you so many stories of her life.

I am ambitious for myself and for the people I love. I question myself every day, but keep going. You cannot be afraid to make mistakes or fail. I learn from others daily and, in return, I like to share my knowledge with others. My motto is: seize the day. Be loyal to your values. Do not mistake determination with stubbornness. You may be demanding, but not rude. Over the years, I have learned to be more patient and flexible. You learn by watching.

Daphné Hézard

Her Monaco youth was spent surrounded by high-octane elegance, but Daphné Hézard's greatest influence came from her mother's wholesome roots, which now inform an appreciation for purposeful, utilitarian design. As the globetrotting fashion director of *Monocle* magazine, based between London and Paris, Hézard enjoys uncovering the stories of artisan businesses, old and new. And her downtime pleasures also come from the small but special things – handmade knitwear, flea-market foraging or a scenic jog in the park.

I don't know if my parents were the most stylish people, but they had a natural lifestyle elegance. My father was keen on English cars and, when driving and walking, would always be accompanied by his little fox terrier. When my mum met my dad, they decided to open a menswear business.

Growing up in Monaco I was surrounded by the Mediterranean Sea, so nature and the crowd there inspired me more than the catwalks or the fashion shoots. My mother comes from the mountains, where it's rough and beautiful: the houses, the woods – simple things with lots of values. I was inspired by that part of my family; utilitarian style, like backpacks, rather than really fancy dressing.

When I was young I wasn't so interested in fashion. But then my sister and I started reading French *Elle* and the original version of French *Glamour*, during the early years of Juergen Teller and Carine Roitfeld. When we went on holiday to London, we would want to know all the good places to go; that's probably how I became curious about fashion.

I appreciate the beauty of simple things and masterpieces. I'm quite nostalgic, so I like old things that remind me of something. Sometimes I'll go to the flea market where they have some amazing pieces, but I will always like the one simple thing that's not for sale.

When I go to the country I always love the outfits of people, like the farmers or the gauchos in Argentina. I would do anything to buy the trousers they're wearing! I like traditional things but mixed with modern.

I go to the flea market almost every Sunday in the winter. I really love it; it's something I associate with winter. At home in Paris, I have a marble-top desk, it's an old bank's table from Les Puces de Clignancourt.

On my desk is a photograph of me by the Argentinian artist, Irina Werning. You give her a picture of you as a kid and she shoots you in exactly the same position with the same clothes and the same expression as when you were 8 years old. If you have a special jumper knitted by your grandmother, she will knit the same jumper. It was a project I did with her for the ninetieth anniversary of *L'Officiel* when I was the editor.

I work in the fashion industry but I'm not the biggest consumer. I prefer to buy one unique, very good quality product from a Scottish brand still producing it from their mills somewhere. Since working at *Monocle*, I really appreciate the Italian know-how, the British know-how, the idea of 'Made in France'. It's very important to me to know where the product comes from and how it's made. I'd rather have things that last.

We know that girls can wear menswear, men can wear womenswear; but men wearing lace stuff, I don't like so much. It's just provocation. The question of gender has been over-discussed and, while I've been happy to wear menswear over the past few years, I have to say I'm starting to reconsider the question. I want to go back to a more feminine style.

My favourite pieces are the handmade clothes, knitted for me. They're priceless because they don't exist anywhere else.

With beauty, I'm always quite feminine. I have long hair, I wear lipstick sometimes and, often, I have red nails. I love to use Tata Harper skincare products. And I like strong perfume. I wear Shalimar by Guerlain and I love Coriandre, and Keora, from Jean Couturier – they're almost impossible to find any more though. I also wear newer brands like Comme des Garçons; they have a perfume called Daphne that I use.

My simple pleasure is jogging in the morning in the Jardin des Plantes in Paris, or in London in Green Park. I like to see the beauty of the city in Paris and the magnificence of the parks in London. It's an effort as well as a pleasure.

I like to use my *Monocle* diary and I always have a notebook. Notebooks are very important for me, because I write all the time. And I keep them all.

I was given the opportunity to start working very young, at 17 years old, and for the best companies I could have imagined working for at that age. When you're young, people like to teach you, train you and to take you under their wing. [*Monocle* founder] Tyler Brûlé was my first boss when he started *Wallpaper* magazine. Then I worked with Joseph Ettedgui, at Joseph, where I had a good position for my age as a PR assistant. I also worked for Vivienne Westwood and I was made editor of *Jalouse* and *L'Officiel*.

I have travelled a lot but now, in my thirties, I also think it's nice to settle a bit, otherwise you're always escaping. It's nice to have a routine, to stay in the same place and to slow down.

Phyllis Wang

Comedienne, fashion collaborator and frequent traveller, Phyllis Wang has never had a plan. Instead, the Taiwanese-American-in-Paris lets her instincts guide her, in life and work, while her dry wit and magnetic energy can't help but attract equally unconventional spirits. An ardent supporter of creative artisans, her arts education continues to inform her taste, whether that's an appreciation of Chinese sculpture or a fetish for Thomas Tait's luxury leather jackets.

I was born in New York but raised mainly in Los Angeles, California. I had a normal, upper-middle-class Taiwanese-American upbringing where my father was a businessman and my mother was a homemaker. I went to very good private schools and, when I graduated from Berkeley, I focused on art history and also theatre. I went to drama school in London and during that time I was also doing quite a few things in fashion.

My fashion relationship has always been instinctual. When you meet people in different situations there's an energy and there's an interest. I don't know how to separate them. The energy is also reflected in how you dress and that attracts like-minded people. It's really from those experiences that I ended up doing different things.

When I started comedy, it was actually by talking to some guy at a party. We were having a 'tit for tat' about something and a friend of mine was like, 'You know, Phyllis, you have a very wry, dry sense of humour, you should think about stand-up.'

My father was quite stylish and so is my mum. She used to buy a lot of Donna Karan. She never worked in an office, it was just an aesthetic she really liked and appreciated. It was through both of them that I found a sense of my own taste.

My father was always really interested in Chinese art. He collected a lot of bronzes, paintings and ceramics and I think I was influenced by his love of Asian culture and also art. When you're studying art history in the States, they have a very European focus. For them it's Western art history that is 'art'. But, with my background, it's only one of the arts. Different cultures have their own evolution of art and aesthetics and so I did both.

I do love my clothes! When I shop, whether it's a vintage shop or a grandma shop or a high-street label or a luxury brand, it's really the details and the workmanship and the form that I'm totally into.

I love Thomas Tait leather jackets. I used to think Junya Watanabe did the best leather jackets but then when Thomas came about I was like, 'Wow, this guy does the best leathers.' His take on the Perfecto is super-unique.

I remember a friend of mine saying, 'You really need to stop wearing this intellectual, architectural bullshit. No guy's going to want you if you dress like that.' Maybe it was my prudish Asian side but it never dawned on me to dress for a man. I always just dressed how I felt.

When I'm living with something, I have to like it. Most of the things I have are based on both function and aesthetics. I wouldn't say it's only aesthetics; I think I'm more on the path of whatever works, works. I have a lot of furniture that my mother gave me, and things like that, that aren't my taste but they have become a part of my life. It's emotional and practical.

A really big part of what stand-up comedians do, we'll constantly have a notebook and we're jotting down different ideas. It's a constant process. Always observing the world around you and, also, the world inside of you in relation to the world around you. There's a certain sense of understanding yourself.

I make an effort to make some time to write every day. And I'm not even saying, 'OK, you have to be funny.' I'm just saying, 'OK, Phyllis, write what is inside of you and, if you have to, make it funny after.' Or, if it's just letting it out, then that's OK as well.

If I like something I'll probably buy it. I don't know if it's because I'm older but I find that I like things less and less. I'm being a bit choosier and in a way it's a great thing. I like to think that, because I choose everything, it is a conscious form of consumption.

My mother taught me it's really important to take care of your skin. I veer towards organic skincare products. I always go back to Dr. Hauschka and I have a lot of essential oils; I have oils for the chakras. I'm not very knowledgeable about Ayurvedic medicine, but I do find that the smells

of the essential oils do different things to me. It's mainly about the skin: it reflects how you feel. I find when my skin is horrible it's because I'm not feeling so great. It's not living, it's not full of life.

I really like going across the street and having a coffee at the bar. If I'm working on editing material, then just being around other people is quite nice. Paris is great for that. It has a café culture, which I really like.

There are moments I really enjoy being around people and I find the exchange and the engagement, even on social media, very nourishing. But I cannot live just on that. I need moments when I can just be within myself, by myself. And so, after travelling a lot, there's a moment when I need to be in one place at one time and focus. Sometimes we can spread ourselves too thin and it's the nature of the modern world.

I actually have quite a large collection of DVDs and, yeah, I could watch them on Netflix but I also like that I have a library of DVDs like I have a library of books. I have a lot of novels, philosophical books and psychology books. And I have a lot of Freud books: he wrote a whole volume on comedy. Every time I'm really into something I'm, like, 'I need a book about that.' Maybe that's my way of consuming it. I need to know about it by reading about it before I feel like I know anything.

Not everything you do in life will be successful, but that's how it is. And, actually, that's part of why we continue. Sometimes I feel like, for me, comedy is about changing the way people think, through laughter. It's not just cracking one joke after the other. If I want to get to that place I'm going to have to go through moments where I'm not going to crack the laugh. Not everything we do will be successful and it's quite a good journey in order to do what we want.

Laurence Dacade

A shoe-obsessed, houseboat-dwelling Parisienne, Laurence Dacade is the creative and business brains behind her eponymous brand. Running her own line while consulting for some of the most influential luxury brands, her love of transformation and hands-on craft infuses everything she does – from reappropriating vintage men's shoes, to upcycling former samples into 'sculptures'. But look past the creative aesthete and there's an equal passion for practicality, in which the importance of comfort can't be underestimated.

Art was very important in my family. My father is obsessed with paintings and my family are keen collectors and spent time acquiring and auctioning art. They introduced me to different types of art – modern art and old paintings, as well as furniture and even old jewellery.

Shoes were my passion but it took time to discover that my passion could also be my job. My father had his own business and his work and his passion were two separate things for him, so I thought your passion was something you had to keep for yourself and not share with people.

When I started my company, it was very important to me to build it in the right way. As a designer I had to face new areas such as the legal, the financial and other technical aspects. I completely involved myself in the project to make it sustainable, surrounded by people I trust. I learned to place confidence in my own convictions and anticipate situations. It's a difficult job and you have to work a lot for sure, but if you do it with love, and you like it, other people like it too, so it works.

I work everywhere. Let's say I have many 'offices' in my home! It's spread out everywhere but, for me, it's organized. There are sketches, leather, colour cards, pencils and you'll see shoes everywhere, even places that they're not supposed to be. There are shoes I designed for previous haute couture clients and shoe sculptures in various places, made of samples that have never been worn. I keep them in the living room and even in the bathroom.

My bathroom has plenty of shoes, books, objects and my Asian art collection, because I don't like my bathroom to look like a bathroom.

We live on a boat and these days we're doing more around the water. We have a moored boat and one with a motor, so we can go on the Seine, or just relax around the boat. We also go water-skiing, which I love.

Transformation is something that I really like. Sometimes I'll find something at the flea market and I'll make it into something that it's not necessarily supposed to be used for. I used to do much more of that – lots of paintings and collage, stitching and gluing things. I have to confess that I need to do things with my hands a lot. I also like doing things with my children. I like when they are creative and when they want to transform something.

My favourite places to shop are in London, New York and Los Angeles. There are great places for vintage and especially vintage shoes. But, when I buy vintage shoes, I don't buy the beautiful ones; I need them to be ugly because otherwise you just want to copy them. It's more about the leather, or the stitches, or I like the technique. It's good to interpret and to mix and transform things.

The most important thing for me is to have comfort in your shoes. It's something very sensual. I never wear socks in winter, for example, because I need to feel the leather inside the shoes. You feel the luxury, the shape, everything you don't see is just as important.

I don't like obvious sexiness but I like sensuality, which I find in masculinity and femininity mixed together. For example, my pants are from the Comme des Garçons men's collection, which I bought in the smallest size. They're still really baggy but I like that. They're grey with stripes and black embroidery - in fact, they're quite feminine men's trousers. Also, when men wear something a bit feminine, I think this can be elegant too. It depends who you are and how you wear the clothes.

I like the way men's clothes and shoes are manufactured. In one of my collections I have a lot of shoes like that; they were made in a men's factory. But I don't like when things are too masculine, because I like to be a woman.

Perfume is my second passion. I put it all around my house - I need to smell something every minute. When I'm working, I use lots of scented candles and I have a big collection of perfumes, mainly around amber, tobacco and patchouli and all those notes.

Sophie Auster

From early beginnings singing in the school choir and studying drama in London, Sophie Auster found her niche as a singer–songwriter. Her formative style influence came from her mother, the writer Siri Hustvedt, whose elegant, androgynous wardrobe now inspires Auster's signature stage uniform of vintage trouser suits. With a tough work attitude entwined with a love for nostalgia and storytelling, this history geek spends her downtime enjoying art-house movies or revelling in the grand beauty of the New York Public Library.

I was always interested in style and clothes. I was a theatrical child so, as an up-and-coming performer, I was always jumping into different costumes and was very interested in changing the perception of myself through things I put on. I also have an extremely elegant mother who was completely well-dressed at all times.

I think it was my mum who started the androgynous appeal for me. She's a writer and she's also very involved with the neuroscience community, which are considered serious occupations. The way you dress gives off a kind of perception. You don't want to dress in a way that conveys that you're not taking something seriously. So my mother wore a lot of beautiful high-waisted pants, and collars and little sweaters, and was just very put together, but never too feminine. That was something that I thought was really attractive.

In my everyday life, I straddle that line between feminine and masculine, and especially on stage

I go way into a more androgynous look, with lots of suits and stuff that is going to make me feel in charge rather than vulnerable. I would say it's almost like a shield, being suited up. You feel strong in it and I like to feel that way, especially on stage.

I'm a musician so I'm usually on a tight budget. The most fun I have shopping at this point is for on-stage clothing. I think very carefully about what I want to say, because a red velvet suit and a ribbon tie says something, instead of just a pair of jeans and a T-shirt. I found my Tom Ford for Gucci velvet suit at a vintage store in New York. It was just one of those crazy things. And I'm lucky that a lot of vintage clothes fit me pretty well, so I didn't have to do anything to it.

When I'm consuming and buying things it's to have something that will be very special. I tend to go to a lot of vintage stores because there's a sense of history and something much more unique. I have this lawn dress from 1880 that I love because, every time I put it on, I imagine some girl from long ago in her garden wearing this dress. I like having pieces where you can picture those sorts of scenarios.

I never want to look like I'm wearing too much make-up. It's all very light; I like the 'no make-up' make-up look. Laura Mercier and Chanel make-up are good for my dry skin. And a skin oil is nice: I use one from Skin Laundry.

Anything you put in your apartment or on your body is you presenting to the world, 'This is who I am'. In my apartment I have lots of personal photos and artwork and stuff from family and friends. There's a big collage on my wall, lots of instruments and a record console. It feels very much like me.

One of my most meaningful possessions is a drawing given to me when I was 8 years old. My father was judging the Cannes Film Festival that year and, needless to say, I really didn't know what I was doing there. So I spent a lot of hours at tables with a lot of grown-ups, drawing, and one of those evenings I happened to sit next to Tim Burton. He felt equally as bored as I was and he engaged me in this long conversation and was very, very interested in all the sketches I was doing. The next day, he delivered a watercolour drawing of Edward Scissorhands and I have that framed on my wall (opposite, below right).

I started singing at 8 years old in the school choir. And then, theatre came into my life through singing and I liked both, but I didn't know exactly what I was going to be. It's kind of amazing that I have become a songwriter because, growing up, I thought that I was going to be a musical actress. I thought, 'Well there's the perfect combination: I like performing, I love singing, I can also act but I'm not going to be necessarily writing my own material.'

I'm always going after something, I'm very aggressive. I wasn't always like that but the more you focus, the more you understand how much you want something and that no one's going to do it for you. You really have to push yourself along and, yes, it can be excruciating sometimes because you come up against people who don't care who you are; they're just thinking about the money they may or may not make. That can be a blow to your ego but, at the same time, I don't care, because most of the time they can be jerky about it, or they can just say yes or no. That's the chance you take.

One of my simple pleasures is going to see a movie with a friend at the Film Forum in New York. Those kinds of theatres only attract people who really want to go to the movies. It's a very quiet, appreciative audience; everyone claps at the end of the film and you feel like you're really part of some kind of community.

The New York Public Library is one of the most beautiful places to visit. I'm a real sucker for history and walking into places where you feel very small. You look up and you think about all these very old texts and it's such a beautiful building, it gives you a real sense of perspective. Maybe I'm a nerd but it makes me kind of excited.

Kristen Naiman

Storytelling through style is the default mode of Kristen Naiman. From her role as vice-president of brand creative at Kate Spade New York, to her love of sentimental jewellery and blue-and-white china, there's meaning and self-expression at the heart of everything she does. As a founding partner of elevated basics line Apiece Apart, this rigorous editor is also a champion of intelligent style who is happiest in a Charvet button-down shirt and classic Manolo Blahnik heels.

I think that style is innate. There are people who grow up steeped in the environment of it and there are people who are intuitively attracted to it, find it and seek it out in whatever environment they grow up in. I'm somewhere in the middle.

At Kate Spade, I oversee everything you see that tells the story of the brand in all its iterations. To me, clothes are always connected to the story, and culture, and self-expression. I know that people use clothes to describe themselves and I describe the brand to the rest of the world.

For someone who does what I do, I'm a strong editor. I like to get rid of things. As I've moved on in life and deepened my connection with style, there's a practical part of me that just wants to buy classic things that last a really long time.

I'm happiest in a man's button-down shirt. I buy them from all different places across the board, from Uniqlo to Charvet. I like J.Crew men's shirts. They're a little more affordable but they're still pretty good, certainly compared to Charvet, for example.

One of my favourite movies is a documentary by Agnès Varda, called *The Gleaners And I*, about the value of things that have been discarded. I always think about that when I'm in consignment stores: this idea that though something's no longer useful to one person, to another person it's a gem. To me, that has a lot of value and specialness to it.

I'm pretty much always in a heel because I wear very boyish things a lot of the time. I look for simplicity but boldness, so I love a straight-up plain Manolo Blahnik pointy-toed pump – there's a crispness to that that pulls everything together. But I also love my Charlotte Olympia sandals with a big red piece of coral on them.

My favourite item is a Junya Watanabe cape that's navy blue and has two closures and no armholes, but it's beautiful and super-simple. I also have a Sacai dress that has a tie at the back and wraps at the waist – it's really timeless.

With Apiece Apart, we were thinking about the idea that you have this interlocking core of feminine, intelligent pieces, and they could be the *tabula rasa* for the slightly more adventurous things that you buy along the way. The formula that's key for us is the combination of strength of silhouette and making sure the silhouette is always classic and yet always timely.

I like jewellery that means something to me and I like jewellery that I can wear every single day. I have two brass bracelets that a friend of mine makes that I've had forever and a watch I wear that was made for Isaac Mizrahi, where I worked for eight years. It's my favourite watch and it reminds me of all the time that I spent there when I look at it. Then I have a ring that I had made with my initial and my daughter's initial, and another ring that was a baby ring that my mom made for my sister. And then I wear a few bangles from Kate Spade. I wear all of those every day and I never ever think about it.

My beauty routine is very stripped back. There's usually a body scrub, there's one hair product, there's a moisturizer and I like cheap Maybelline mascara. My signature beauty item is definitely my red lipstick and there really is no other thing. I have no anti-line thing, I don't use powder; I'm very streamlined about it.

I was in college before there was email, so I have a fundamentally old-fashioned feeling of privacy that I maintain in a way that maybe isn't in keeping with our social-media times. That said, there's something empowering about the idea that social media allows everybody who's interested in one specific thing to huddle around it. It allows for things to have much more currency in the world so, by specializing, you actually democratize the idea of creativity.

I love working with other people, seeing what interests them, what motivates them and how to inspire them. I find all of that fascinating. I am a tough boss; I'm demanding and I'm an insane perfectionist, but I do also really, really like people.

I love to walk and I often take a more direct subway to a further-away place from my house and walk home from the subway. Sometimes I'm talking on the phone, other times I'm just thinking, but I like the moving and the speed of walking, as opposed to running or riding a bike.

I collect blue-and-white china. I like the fact that it's universal: I have Japanese, I have some Swedish, but I don't collect it excessively. I don't like to have tons of it; I like the thought and what it means to me. I don't collect it for the collecting: I collect it for the thinking and for the economy of it. It allows me to have a kind of guardrail [crash barrier]. The way to connect to it is deeper than just, 'Oh, how pretty!'

Functional, beautiful and adaptable, those are the requirements of the garconne's hardest-working wardrobe components. Here's why they're important, where to buy the best examples and how to make them your own.

The Style Codes

CHAPTER 3

The Overcoat

'I feel happiest in a well-cut coat. The weight of the fabric, the silhouette, it's the difference between the flabby cut of a coat, and one that's cut really sharply and neatly.' So says Donna Wallace, accessories editor of *Elle* (see page 48) and an excellent advert for how to wear a great coat. Wallace favours trad-looking overcoats, but with an unexpected detail – an exaggerated furry collar say, or an elaborate embroidered sleeve.

When it comes to masculine overcoats, all roads lead to Crombie, the British men's outerwear stalwarts. Originating in 1805, and supplying cloth and uniforms to the American and British armies, the close-tailored three-quarter-length coats became popular with English gents,

political powerhouses and Hollywood greats, including John F. Kennedy and Cary Grant. These days, the Crombie cut is regularly referenced by the likes of Prada, Raf Simons and Ralph Lauren, both in menswear and womenswear, for its refined, presence-commanding appeal.

But it's the newer designers who make it their own: Thomas Tait and Christopher Kane have become known for covetable overcoats, while A. Sauvage represents the new wave of gender-neutral coat design.

Aside from Donna Wallace, my other favourite overcoat wearers include model and music producer Caroline de Maigret, writer Fran Lebowitz and jeweller Gaia

Repossi; add to those anyone in a Bruce Weber shoot. As with masculine trousers, a personal flourish of femininity is always a welcome part of the mix, whether that's an heirloom bracelet watch, four-inch-heeled snakeskin boots or a stain of matte pink lipstick.

For colour and detail: **Paul Smith, Dries Van Noten**

For affordability: **Whistles, J.Crew, & Other Stories, Filippa K** (above)

The Trousers

French women seem to be adept at demonstrating the art of the expertly cut trouser. Style setters Inès de la Fressange, Garance Doré and Charlotte Gainsbourg all excel at wonderful trouser-wearing.

The magic is in the cut and the fabric, namely, a streamlined cut with a blade-sharp crease and a natural waist. I like a slim, cropped, cigarette trouser, but even a fuller peg-legged cut can look streamlined if it's cut properly. Never put anything in your pockets – pocket bulges are a sartorial sin of the highest order! And go for the best fabric you can afford: it will just hang better.

I'm not a fan of too much stretch in tailored trousers. As with other menswear-inspired pieces, they're so much better when they're not messed about with. So aim for wool gabardine, flannel, or wool crepe for evening. Splash out on just one pair of impeccable, classic-cut pants like these and know that you can reach for them any time you really want to feel in charge.

Should you be fortunate enough to afford it, it's worth having a pair made bespoke. Former Chloé creative director Hannah MacGibbon heads to Savile Row suit-makers Anderson & Sheppard or Henry Rose. Once you have had the first pattern cut, you're set with a template for life.

Off-the-peg masculine styles look alluringly feminine when partnered with their opposite number: pleated mousseline blouses, bare-toed stilettos, a delicate watch or a vintage ring. But, once you've nailed the basic cut, feel free to go as wild as you like on colour, texture and print.

For classic cuts: **Céline**, **Maison Margiela**, **Joseph** (above), **Balenciaga**

The Sweater

Ever since Coco Chanel famously co-opted her lover's cosy cardigans, we've had our own affair with cashmere and traditional Scottish-made knitwear. Fittingly, in 2012, Chanel bought the Hawick-based Barrie Knitwear company, the better to produce its own luxurious sweaters, widely recognized as among the best in the world.

Let's be clear: cashmere mostly comes from China, sourced from the underbelly of Mongolian goats, with the longest, whitest, thinnest hairs being transported to Scotland and Italy for spinning, dyeing and knitting. Those affordable made-in-China cashmeres you find on the high street aren't bad, but the raw material is likely to be shorter, coarser hair, or even combined with rabbit hair. And the quality differential often extends to the finished garment – a fluffy surface or too-stretchy sweater is a telltale sign of a false economy that will, sooner rather than later, pill endlessly or lose its shape. To be safe, look for Scottish-made cashmere.

While good cashmere is undoubtedly the loveliest sort of knitwear, Merino wool is its sensible little sister for trans-seasonal dressing or warmer climates. Fine-gauge Merino knits have a flattering drape whether they're slouchy in cut or fitted, and are, of course, infinitely more affordable.

What I also love about Merino knits is their layering potential. Shrunken-fitting sweaters slide easily under slim-shouldered jackets, while oversized ones can be thrown readily over shirts, blouses and dresses without adding bulk. If you prefer your knits on the roomy side, look in the menswear departments. The cut tends to be more classic and the prices are usually better too.

For Merino knits: **Céline**, **Bella Freud**, **John Smedley**, **Uniqlo**

For Scottish quality: **Johnstons of Elgin**, **Margaret Howell**

For new design: **&Daughter** (above), **ESK Cashmere**

The Flat Shoes

When it comes to getting things done, a gentlewoman relies on good shoes. And, very often, those are shoes with a legacy: the Oxford, the brogue, the loafer. Such classics may be borrowed from the gentleman, but they're worn with a woman's unique stylistic spin. When these shoes are teamed with equally boyish tailored suits or trousers, I immediately think of Katharine Hepburn's insouciance and Janelle Monáe's dramatic presence.

But that's not the only way to wear them. Sturdy masculine shoes almost look better when contrasted with the soft and romantic, hence I love the idea of heavy brogues worn with a djellaba-like shirt dress, or Bermuda shorts and a cotton-voile blouse.

For a good investment, handmade shoes can't be beaten. It takes no less than 250 manual steps to build a pair of Church's brogues, a process that takes up to eight weeks. Grenson, another British shoemaker, has been manufacturing its brogues and Oxfords since 1866, using the Goodyear Welting process, which allows shoes to be resoled several times, making the investment go further.

Loafers have a special place in my heart and those by heritage French brand J.M. Weston (above) are crafted in Limoges using an ancestral tanning method that gives a superb rich finish. And I'm eternally on the hunt for vintage, dead-stock Bass Weejuns loafers, better looking and better built than today's equivalents.

Is it worth buying the fashion version of a gentleman's shoe? Sure, especially if you want something a bit livelier in colour or detail.

For updated classics: **Paul Smith**

For avant-garde detail: **Prada, Marni, Comme des Garçons**

The Watch

We all know that watches aren't essential accoutrements these days, yet that doesn't stop us wanting them. Until now, the bulk of the $50-billion Swiss watch industry has been aimed at the moneyed masculine market but, as sales dipped, the realization dawned that women love buying luxury watches for themselves.

'I stopped wearing a watch when I joined Tank. I think it was my rebellion against my management background. But, now I realize watches are a whole territory of accessories that one can explore,' says Tank Group CEO Caroline Issa (see page 36). 'I've got my eye on a 1950s Rolex that I saw on an Italian woman, which she'd put on a ribbon. And one day I think I'd treat myself to a Cartier Tank.'

It's no surprise that classics such as the Cartier Tank or Hermès Cape Cod are so popular. They don't shout, they're versatile and they come in enough variations that you can make one your signature. Alternatively, Chanel's Boy.Friend watch epitomizes the new breed of understated, masculine-looking timepieces. Away from these stealth-luxe watches, there's plenty of demand for statement-makers. The Hermès Médor, a showstopper of pyramid studs on a leather band based on the humble dog collar, originated in 1993 and is as popular as ever.

But it's not just expensive new watches that appeal to discerning timekeepers. Hand-me-down watches can be emotional objects, connecting the wearer

to a relative or an important moment in time. And vintage watches are often better made and longer-lasting than new. On the high street, the democratic Swatch watch continues to be much loved thanks to a myriad of designs, old and new. Shinola is a recent entry to the mid-price market, with its trad-looking Runwell (above), while Uniform Wares is another relative newcomer, with its anonymous-looking unisex watches coveted by the design and architecture set.

For timeless luxury: **Cartier**, **Hermès**

For everyday utility: **Swatch**, **Uniform Wares**

The Raincoat

Despite its practicality, there's something rather beautiful and romantic about the raincoat. Perhaps it's the vision of Audrey Hepburn drenched but comforted in the arms of George Peppard in *that* scene from *Breakfast at Tiffany's*. Or simply my own experience when properly protected in Burberry's finest trench, come the inevitable London downpour.

Fashion raincoats can look tatty, not stylish, after constant wear. So if your mac is going to get regularly saturated, it's worth shelling out for the best (read: 'indestructible') you can afford.

Burberry and Mackintosh are the greats because they're built for protection. The story goes that the British World War I War Office commissioned Burberry to update its Tielocken raincoat, with its epaulettes and D-rings, to create the now familiar trench. It's quite remarkable how little the original design has changed.

Meanwhile, the company we know as Mackintosh created the first rubber-coated raincoat in 1823, and these highly water-repellent macs have evolved into simple, yet fashion-forward, colours and designs that are often commissioned by the world's luxury brands. In recent years, another player has joined the rainwear game: Hancock's founder, Daniel Dunko, was responsible for the noughties Mackintosh revival and is bringing the same technical innovation and handcraft to a new generation of outerwear.

Functionality aside, sometimes it's the look, rather than the utility of a mac that appeals – blame it on all those impossibly cool 1960s Parisian students. And for some reason, classic macs are abundant in the world's thrift stores. The beauty of this timeless staple is that the fit needn't be perfect. So feel free to make it your own, with upsized proportions, upturned collar, rolled sleeves and a cashmere scarf.

For modern classics: **Margaret Howell, A.P.C., agnès b., Paul Smith** (above)

The Handbag

The garconne's multifaceted lifestyle demands a bag for every situation. Not hundreds, but enough of an edit to fulfil practical requirements, as well as satisfying beauty and style needs.

Many of the best-loved heritage brands originated with saddlery and luggage. These utilitarian leather-goods houses use the best leathers and ancient stitching techniques to build bags that will likely outlive their owners. Hermès, Louis Vuitton, Goyard, Delvaux and Moynat are steeped in craft and provenance, and have become newly fashionable thanks to a better-informed consumer.

Of the more contemporary handbag brands, simplicity of design tends to have

everlasting appeal. I love the throw-it-all-in totes from Anya Hindmarch, Valextra and Céline: both the structured styles for safely toting tech accessories and the softer bags for weekend exploits.

A wave of affordable entries to the classic-bag arena includes Mansur Gavriel's bucket bags, which are vegetable-tanned in small batches, a process that delivers stunning colour saturation. And the pebble-grained bags from Milli Millu take knocks and bumps easily, while keeping their refined good looks.

Everyday bags aside, everyone should have one trophy bag to show off her taste. According to Fanny Moizant, co-founder of luxury consignment site, Vestiaire

Collective, a vintage Hermès or Chanel handbag is the canniest of investments. Recently reworked from its original 1969 design, the Hermès Constance has had a surge in popularity – find a vintage one in excellent condition and it could fetch more at resale than its new equivalent.

For enduring appeal: **Bally** (above), **Chanel**, **J&M Davidson**, **Hermès**

The Trouser Suit

Since the 1990s, the most enduring suit-cut has been the one that that decade defined: think Helmut Lang's, Ann Demeulemeester's and Jil Sander's minimalist, androgynous proportions. Neither too curvy nor too boxy, it has a gently tapered trouser which is sometimes a little cropped to allow a variation of heel heights.

Masculine tailoring flits in and out of fashion but a modified version of it recognizes a woman's shape without obviously emphasizing it. It's why women still covet the original Saint Laurent tuxedo, why Hedi Slimane's slimline boys' suits were stolen by girls during his time at Dior Homme, and why his women's tuxedos at Saint Laurent are sell-outs.

If you're buying a suit with classic proportions, you may as well invest in the best you can afford – the difference in cut and cloth will be worth it. If money's no object, go for bespoke or made to measure from Savile Row, or Edward Sexton (who helped Stella McCartney establish her signature cut) in Knightsbridge. At Pallas, husband-and-wife duo Daniel Pallas and Véronique Bousquet have been stealthily producing prototype samples for the likes of Céline and now create their own line of streamlined suits in hot pink and ivory.

To loosen up a suit, I like an undone element or two. Casual hair, a fine-gauge knit in lieu of a shirt, a lived-in brogue with bare ankles, or even a simple tennis shoe; they all have a charm that's cool and feminine.

For luxury classics: **Ralph Lauren, Paul Smith**, **Jil Sander**, **Acne Studios**

For affordable quality: **A.P.C.**, **Joseph**, **J.Crew**, **Helmut Lang** (above)

The Shirt

Why has something as pedestrian as a white shirt achieved god-like status in stylish circles? I'd hazard a guess that it's down to the uniform-like simplicity that allows endless interpretations and styling options. Not to mention its magical qualities as a light reflector of sorts, imparting a lit-from-within glow to the face. And there's also the history; who hasn't looked great in a Great White Shirt? From the Gibson Girl in her pie-frilled collar, to Patti Smith's déshabillé garconne shirt, it has a rich history to mine for references.

There are other shirts in other colours, such as the kaleidoscope of silk Equipment ones (above) that really do live up to the old day-to-night, work-to-weekend cliché; or M.i.H. Jeans's horn-buttoned Chambray classics; or the voluminous statement-makers from Atlantique Ascoli that have a whiff of luxe artist's smock, in camel and black cotton-linen faille.

Proportions are key, with loose, mannish cuts being the most comfortable to wear. Let's not forget that Margaret Howell began with her line of men's shirts; as did Dries Van Noten, who famously scaled down his men's shapes for a capsule line of women's shirts back in 1986. In this case, it doesn't hurt to reveal a little skin. M.i.H. Jeans founder Chloe Lonsdale instinctively rolls her sleeves to highlight a delicate wrist, all the better for showing off simple accessories – a treasured watch,

for example, or single architectural cuff. Formal occasions may call for a slimmer shirt in a precise cut, which is where the custom-made Charvet shirt comes in. Coco Chanel was frequently seen in her custom Charvets, while director Sofia Coppola buys hers in bulk to wear on film shoots. But, happily, there are excellent shirts to be found on a less luxurious budget, from the Brooks Brothers kids' department, COS and Gap.

For high-street budgets: **Inès de la Fressange for Uniqlo, J.Crew menswear**

The Dress

For the grown-up garconne, the ideal dress is easy, comfortable and far from frou-frou. So it tends to be either a minimalist feat of architectural engineering (something tailored from Maison Margiela, Balenciaga or Yang Li), or a soft, smock-like garment that owes its origin to the shirt.

Fabric is of the utmost importance, as these dresses have to feel good. Egg, Margaret Howell and Comme des Garçons excel in crisp, papery cottons and linens that get better with age. For the kind of straight, long-sleeved shift you find at COS, thick crepe or wool gabardine help add structure, while, at the conceptual end of the scale, modern technical fabrics also have sculptural

properties as well as surface detail (don't be alarmed, today's polyester blends are nothing like their 1970s relatives).

There are other essential considerations, namely proportions and pockets. For La Garçonne's in-house Moderne line, pockets add to the relaxed demeanour of a dress (mainly for hands though, not office paraphernalia, and definitely not for heavy or sticky-outy things such as phones). On a tailored dress, the shoulders and sleeves benefit from precise proportions. The shoulders need to be just so, while sleeves should never be longer than wrist-bone length. Get these elements right and your dress will look and feel like it was made with you in mind.

For everyday versatility: **Dries Van Noten, Burberry** (above)

For feel-good fabrics: **Egg, Margaret Howell, Comme des Garçons**

The Intimates

When Gabrielle Chanel and her garconne cohorts ushered in loose-fitting knits and anti-hourglass dresses, they simultaneously sounded the death knell for the corset. In its place came softer underpinnings, epitomized by Hanro's flat-knit viscose camisoles, which were recommended to customers of Chanel's *sportif* designs.

The delicate Hanro 1601 camisole is still considered a classic: made from Swiss mercerized cotton with satin spaghetti straps, it doesn't look indecent under a sheer blouse or V-neck man's sweater. These days, it also comes in wool or silk varieties and the matching cotton knickers score equally high – not too skimpy, not too matronly. They're so fine that there's no hint of bulk under lightweight layers.

For more substantial support, today's dedicated minimalist opts for a structured but unconstricting bra. Once it's on, you can forget about it and carry on with your business. For the less well-endowed, Base Range and Blue Canoe specialize in sporty bandeaus and triangle bras that nod to the simple shapes of 1980s and 1990s dancewear, often using natural and sustainable fabrics. And Land of Women's everyday underwear (above) uses a special power-net fabric that sculpts and supports without the need for wires.

For light coverage: **Hanro, Base Range**

For good support: **Calvin Klein, Donna Karan Intimates, Wacoal**

The Heels

The duality of today's gentlewoman is best demonstrated in her choice of shoes: run-around flats for day (Prada brogues, Superga tennis shoes – take your pick), versus something playful and elevated for night. For classicists, there are the sensible single-soled pumps – ideally with a 10cm (4in) cigarette heel. Gianvito Rossi has made a successful business on the back of these walkable beauties, with just the right pointiness to the toe and slender width of heel, while Dior offers a more skewed version, with updates on its iconic Comma silhouette.

Perhaps unexpectedly, our garconne loves a bit of whimsy in her details. Thus, she's not averse to an unwieldy 'jolie-laide' (beautiful-ugly) platform from time to time. 'I definitely get a lot of pleasure out of high heels and high shoes and I think they're very appealing,' says Bella Freud, who offsets her gamine ensembles with jumbo-soled Célines and Louboutins. 'I'm confident enough in my brain to not worry if I seem like I can hardly walk down the street in a pair of shoes, because I'm enjoying the buzz of wearing them and I don't feel compromised by any of the other stuff.'

For the less maverick, the halfway option presents itself in a straight-heeled pump with some element of surprise decoration – sexy ankle ties from Bionda Castana, perhaps, or colourful animal print from Charlotte Olympia (above). And yes, heels can indeed be comfortable, just ask Manolo Blahnik's faithful customers. Or Caroline Issa, who swears by Paul Andrew: 'He puts in invisible padding so when you're on a high heel it's incredibly comfortable. But it looks super-chic at the same time.'

For classic pumps: **Gianvito Rossi**, **Rupert Sanderson**, **Kurt Geiger**

For whimsical detail: **Manolo Blahnik**, **Paul Andrew**, **Charlotte Olympia**

The Sunglasses

For all her considered practicality, a garconne's relationship with sunglasses is more about stylistic expression than shading her eyes. This is where she gets to show her fun side, injecting colour, decoration and general playfulness to an often function-skewed wardrobe.

Prada eyewear is a particular favourite, marrying the intellectuality of the brand (and Mrs Prada herself) with eccentric styling such as mad curlicues and cat-eye proportions. Miu Miu's glittery frames fall into the same category, as do the delicious offerings – both vintage and new – from Cutler and Gross, whose eyewear is hand-finished in Italy and comes with impeccable after-care service.

On the flip side, there's also an abundance of understated architectural shapes. Céline's chunky black shades have their own cult following, even more so since being lent extra cachet by celebrated writer Joan Didion in a 2015 ad campaign. And then there are Dries Van Noten's sunglasses, which, like his clothes, blend classic styling with unusual details and colours. Karen Walker (above) deserves a mention for expertly marrying wearable shapes with exuberant patterns, perfect for offsetting the most serious of masculine or minimalist outfits.

In the wardrobe of everyday essentials Ray-Ban Wayfarers need no introduction. Whether black or tortoiseshell, they come in a variety of sizes to suit all – consider

them the white tee of the eyewear world. And, for just that little bit of edge and glamour, you can't knock a pair of aviators. Originating from the military (the teardrop shape stems from flight goggles), they can't help but telegraph a certain urban adventurer spirit.

For unisex styling: **Ray-Ban**

For playful glamour: **Dries Van Noten, Karen Walker**

The Jewellery

There are two extremes when it comes to gentlewomanly jewellery preferences. On the one hand, the discreet, personal, everyday pieces – a fine identity bracelet, a charm necklace, a cherished ring. On the other, the saved-up-for wow piece – something Cartier and panther-shaped, for example, or a vintage Deco showstopper clamped over the cuff of a skinny sweater.

I'm all about informal, wearable pieces; they become part of your style and what people remember you for. And that's what has led to the popularity of iconic designs such as the Tiffany T bracelet, the Cartier love bangle or my own signifier, the Dinh Van Menottes necklace with its tiny handcuffs clasp (above).

Recent years have seen the rise of casual fine jewellery as a consequence of women buying jewellery for themselves. It's a factor in the success of designers such as Monique Péan (her conflict-free rough-luxe diamond and recycled-gold earrings are a favourite of Caroline Issa) as well as the thoroughly modern offerings from luxury giants. It's really about reimagining the idea of classics, for the denim-and-diamonds set. Staid pearls are anything but, when re-appropriated by Japanese jeweller Tasaki; likewise, the diamond ring when it's one of Repossi's cult Berbère rings, scattered with black diamonds.

The secondary market has become increasingly appealing for the new fine-jewellery buyer, with 1stdibs, eBay and Vestiaire Collective serving as both shopping portals and research resources. Even the legacy auction houses are embracing e-commerce, with Sotheby's teaming up with eBay to sell online. From an investment point of view, it's often a canny move. Buy a vintage heritage piece, rather than the latest 'it' bauble at a similar price, and not only will its rarity make it more special, but its value will also appreciate at the same time too.

For everyday luxury: **Le Gramme**, **Tasaki**, **Repossi**

For vintage gems: **Tiffany**, **Cartier**, **Dinh Van**

The Blazer

Classics are classics because they can't be bettered, and the blazer is a convenient example. It's the linchpin that elevates everything – from jeans and a tee, to a boilersuit, or even a formal gown. As with many classics hijacked from the gentleman's wardrobe, the blazer's heritage is rooted in uniforms – from naval uniforms to those of 1920s tennis players. As such, it was designed as a functional piece of kit, so good construction is vital.

For such a pivotal masterpiece, it's worth spending a bit, which is why I don't hesitate to recommend the structured, slim-shouldered styles offered by Maison Margiela, Stella McCartney, Haider Ackermann and Saint Laurent. Céline is another whose tailored blazer

is a perennial fixture, separate from the headline-grabbers of the catwalk collections. Ralph Lauren and Bouchra Jarrar are worth considering for their more feminine silhouettes, while Louis Vuitton is the go-to brand for slightly undersized proportions. Straight out of Italy, Blazé Milano is a made-to-order line of women's blazers, all handmade from beautiful fabrics.

More affordably, Studio Nicholson is great, because designer Nick Wakeman's menswear background informs her choice of fabrics. J.Crew's offerings (above) also deserve a mention for not straying from the menswear path, as do M.i.H. Jeans's straight-cut, rigid-shouldered blazers. Purists might prefer to shop straight from

the men's department, an easier feat in these times of gender-neutral dressing. In which case, Dior Homme and Paul Smith are good places to start. How to wear it? Don't 'drag up'! Boyish blazers are best worn with an element of softness or sexiness: an unbuttoned blouse, discreet jewellery, a red lip – you get the picture. And, if in doubt, simply ask yourself, 'What would Tilda Swinton do?'

For ultimate luxury: **Saint Laurent**, **Stella McCartney**

For high-street interpretations: **Zara**, **COS**, **Whistles**

The Perfume

Not all garconnes wear fragrance. Many prefer the smell of their own skin, but others relish a scent that they can call theirs. In the last decade, there's been a growth-spurt of artisan fragrance houses, which appeal to the gentlewoman's appreciation for fine artistry. So it's not surprising to note the rise of brands such as Byredo, Nasomatto and Frédéric Malle. Generic drugstore fragrances don't interest the discerning fragrance-wearer, who prefers more complex and unusual fragrances that have individual appeal.

'Women are becoming more aware that there's a world of niche fragrances to explore, rather than just purchasing their usual scent or fashion branded scent,' says Clorinda Di Tommaso of niche fragrance specialists Intertrade. Unisex scents, in particular, appeal to the duality of the New Garconne. The sensual woodiness of Bella Freud's Ginsberg is God and Nasomatto's Pardon are gender-neutral favourites to wear with louche velvet pyjamas or an evening tuxedo. More subtle are the herby notes of a Santa Maria Novella (above) or Hermès cologne.

Experimenting with fragrance-combining can also create new favourites, while the more adventurous can go down the bespoke route. Perfumer Lyn Harris caters for this market with her London atelier, Perfumer H, in which she concocts unique scents for her creative clientele, delivering them in beautiful handblown glass vessels.

These days, fragrance is less about notes and ingredients and more about a multi-sensorial emotion, mood and ritual. It's why shoe designer Laurence Dacade fills her surroundings with a variety of perfumes, using the bottles to decorate her space.

For unisex scent: **Acqua di Parma, Comme des Garçons, Helmut Lang**

For home fragrance: **Diptyque, Fornasetti, Jo Malone London**

The T-shirt

Like a good coat, blazer or well-cut trousers, the T-shirt is one of those wardrobe master pieces that you don't want to have to think too much about. My advice is to repeat-buy the best you can, then you won't have to. Luckily, the brands that make the best tees keep producing them. Agnès b. (above) and Comme des Garçons are my failsafe go-tos for plain, boxy silhouettes that won't cling. They're also built to last; they wear well and don't go wonky in the wash.

For a softer, off-duty tee, I like the ones from Levi's Vintage Clothing which are modelled on an old masculine fit and are a good summer staple for wearing with jeans. (Their long, loose shape is good for achieving the half-in-half-out tuck beloved of certain French fashion editors.) Kids' tees are another secret source – try J.Crew and Petit Bateau – as they tend to be devoid of decoration, bar a pocket or a gentle picot edge.

White tees are my weakness. A semi-circle of bright white tee neckline visible under a dark sweater instantly uplights the face, especially if you're not adventurous with colour. And let's not disregard the ubiquitous striped tee, which always feels so energizing and which is universally flattering. The trick with Bretons and other long-sleeve tees is to roll or fold the sleeves a little, to show some skin and a hint of wristwear.

For the perfect white tee: **agnès b., Comme des Garçons**, **Acne Studios**

For Breton stripes: **Margaret Howell, Petit Bateau**

The Pyjamas

Although faintly ridiculous, there's something endlessly charming about the idea of cocktail pyjamas. Extravagant silk delicacies patterned with a stripe or paisley, they hint at a bygone era of leisure, one that I find particularly seductive in the always-on digital era. Back in the day, Cartier's Jeanne Toussaint wore hers (complete with pearls and turban) at café-society soirées, while Coco Chanel was also a fan, opting for men's pyjamas by Charvet. Originally a shirt maker, Charvet is still serving up Egyptian cottons from its home on Place Vendôme.

Perhaps part of the appeal is the idea that, after your evening of elegant lounging, you can just flop into bed.

There's certainly a relaxed, arty side to pyjama dressing that recalls the bohemian lifestyles of PJ aficionados such as artists David Hockney and Julian Schnabel. As such, old-school mannish pyjamas are enjoying a renaissance, with Olatz Schnabel's jewel-coloured silks and Poplin's crunchy cottons sharing top billing. Equipment, purveyor of everyone's favourite silk shirt, has also branched into pyjama territory, personalizing them with elegant embroidered initials, if so desired. For classicists, Brooks Brothers (above) is still selling the famous cotton pyjamas favoured by Katharine Hepburn, while The Sleep Shirt's traditional offering, in white poplin, is pretty near perfect.

For those who don't live a life of leisure, the artful romance of pyjama dressing can be readily appropriated. I love the wrongness of proper menswear trousers with a jacquard pyjama top, or a pyjama jacket worn undone over a clashing print top. It's a look that Marni, Dries Van Noten and J.Crew regularly revisit to beautiful and dreamy effect.

For masculine classics: **Charvet**, **Brooks Brothers**

For contemporary colour: **Olatz**, **Toast**

The Scarf

The New Garconne rarely overdoses on accessories. Rather, it's about that one well-chosen piece that elevates things almost imperceptibly. Scarves do this well and, in particular, I'm thinking of Hermès men's *cravat foulard*. This long, narrow scarf comes in plain or printed silk and takes zero effort to tie. It has a louche elegance that lends itself to understated blouses or cotton shirts when you want to add something beautiful, yet unfussy.

A step up from those are the rectangular silk scarves that come with polka dots or a frayed edge – the kind at which Margaret Howell (above) excels (especially in navy or dove grey with cream polka dots). Again, these lift a blazer or a coat with their easy, sartorial demeanour.

Of course, I can't talk about scarves without mentioning the Hermès silk square. These are works of art; the colour combinations alone are a lesson in Hermès exactitude and, indeed, they're often collaborations with brilliant artists and colourists. To make it look effortless, it helps to stop trying (and tying) so hard. The trick is not to get caught up in the complexities of scarf-tying origami. Believe me, I've been there. And, after years of frustration, I've realized that the best tactic is to fold diagonally in half, then half tie it loosely around the neck.

Away from the silks, the usefulness of a classic wool, or cashmere, fringed scarf can't be underestimated. From utilitarian neutrals – navy, grey, khaki and camel –

to cherry red, get the biggest you can afford and revel in its all-enveloping warmth and comfort.

For sensual silks: **Hermès, Margaret Howell**

For warmth: **Burberry, Johnstons of Elgin, Marc Jacobs**

The Trainers

Trainers may have become newly fashionable lately, but a certain type of trainer has been a cult classic forever. That trainer is rooted in simplicity and utility, whether it's a no-name white plimsoll, a 1970s-throwback Nike running shoe, a New Balance 576, or the most recent iteration, a Common Projects Achilles leather low-top (above). Everybody's favourite, Converse All Star, started life on the basketball court. Its sporting credentials may be long forgotten but that doesn't stop fetishists hunting down pristine dead-stock supplies from the 1970s. (Look for the 'Made in USA' stamp and the elegant almond-shaped toe.)

Crucially, the cut is a simple one, so we're not talking about Isabel Marant wedge trainers or Rick Owens for Adidas futuristic shenanigans here. If I picture my favourite stylish sports-shoe moment, it's most likely Phoebe Philo in Adidas Stan Smiths or *Elle* magazine's accessories editor Donna Wallace in understated New Balance worn with straight-cut tailored pants and a clean and serene COS sweater.

And that's the crux really; these shoes don't limit you to certain outfits or activities, their anonymity makes them versatile and eminently adaptable. And, understated as they are, they also speak volumes. What do they say? That the wearer likes to get things done, with calm, purposeful efficiency.

For bright whites: **Converse All Star, Converse Jack Purcell, Superga**

For retro running shoes: **Nike, New Balance**

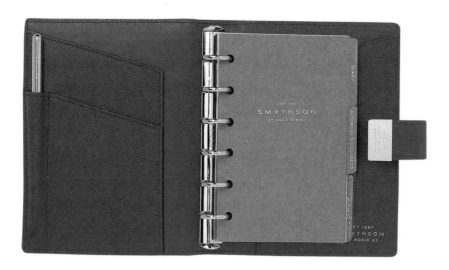

The Stationery

For creative types, it seems that nothing gets those inspirational juices flowing more than putting pencil, pen or brush to paper. However efficient (and omnipresent) our technology, there's a special satisfaction to be found in scribbling dates in a diary or notes in a sketchbook. It's partly to do with the slower pace of gathering thoughts, and partly the added pleasure of archiving these tactile journals to rediscover later.

Many a gentlewoman likes to give and receive a special notebook, preferably leather-bound, possibly initial-stamped. And I'm happy to note that the, admittedly cumbersome but always comforting, leather agenda is alive and well in many desk drawers and cubbyholes.

Mulberry's jumbo organizers are a joy to keep on a desk and use as a never-ending scrapbook, while Anya Hindmarch is the queen of personalizing any and every type of bespoke journal. The Hermès Ulysse notebook, with its pebbled calfskin jacket, takes refills that can be easily installed with the aid of utilitarian press-studs. And Smythson's regal blue-papered diaries and address books have been the choice of discerning women since its inception in 1887.

But fancy leather desk accessories aside, there's a simple pleasure to be had from a cheery Kate Spade notecard or Moleskine notebook. In the end, it's really just about cherishing that fleeting moment to get a thought down on paper before it's gone.

For handcrafted luxury: **Smythson** (above), **Hermès**, **Montblanc**

For spontaneous scribbles: **Kate Spade**, **Moleskine**, **Muji**

The Technology

Gentlewomen agree: today's smart technology is most effective when used as a tool. Yes, the entertainment factor of a smart gadget is high too, but that can be merely another word for distraction. As a life-enabler though, they are indispensable for helping to get things done – fast – and acting as an external hard drive for the overstuffed brain.

Just because an iPhone *can* perform multi-tasking tricks, doesn't mean it should. Emails on-the-go are handy in theory but relentless in practice, so it's best to limit this. The real-life hacks are the apps that filter, edit and organize information so you can locate it when needed, but otherwise forget it. Evernote is one such memory-saver, for filing reams

of work and life documents, instantly findable by tags. Another one is Pocket, which lets you save non-urgent news and articles for a more convenient time, vastly reducing distraction and upping productivity. And Yahoo News Digest keeps you in the loop without sucking you into the internet sinkhole of hell.

For creative entrepreneurs and artists such as Caroline Issa and Polly Morgan, Pinterest and Instagram are the image-sharing apps which, used in moderation for researching and organizing visual ideas, also double as business-promotion tools.

Shopping by social feed is fast replacing the offline boutique browse, thanks to

apps including Lyst, ASAP54, The NET SET and LIKEtoKNOW.it. These let users follow those with similar tastes, a clever shortcut to purposeful shopping. But if all that sounds overwhelming, here's a solution: 'wearable' gadgets, such as the Vinaya smart necklace (above), limit intrusive notifications to the bare essentials, so you're only as connected as you choose to be.

For inspiration: **Instagram**, **Pinterest**, **The NET SET**, **Lyst**

For productivity: **Pocket**, **Evernote**

For downtime: **Headspace**

The Toiletries

As with her clothes, today's careful consumer also has a discerning approach to beauty: once she finds her hero items, the search is off. Endless accumulation is not in keeping with her mind-set (or storage capacity). So what are the keepers of the beauty world for this choosy curator?

Skincare comes first, so facials, serums, double cleansing and SPF prepare the canvas. Linda Rodin's face oils are fetishized for their efficacy and minimalist branding, but pharmacy and spa brands are equally good. I rate Sanctuary Spa's Therapist's Secret Facial Oil and Decléor Neroli Oil Serum, both of which encourage you to give your skin a circulation-boosting massage.

For no-nonsense skincare, Kiehl's and Aēsop (above) share a unisex appeal and handsome, utilitarian looks.

And then there are the bathtime accoutrements that are just that bit more beautiful and indulgent. Yes, it seems extravagant to buy fancy soaps and, yet, I'm a firm believer in the healing effects of a sensorial bathing routine. Santa Maria Novella, founded in 1221, is revered for its natural lotions and soaps. Buly 1803 is similarly appealing. Its pH-neutral, plant-based scented soaps are best bought in person from its delightful Paris apothecary (pick up other artisanal oddities like its green-tea toothpaste while you're there).

For drugstore favourites: **Burt's Bees, Dr. Hauschka, Embryolisse**

For sensual splurges: **Santa Maria Novella, Buly 1803**

The Make-up

Well-looked-after skin generally needs less make-up and, as a fan of great eyebrows, highlighted cheekbones and a red lip, I can say that downsizing your make-up is liberating and allows you to zero in on your favourites.

So, yes, by all means use foundation, concealer and powder if you like to, but apply sparingly. Laura Mercier and Bobbi Brown are the queens of foundation and concealer, while Armani's Luminous Silk foundation is worshipped for its 'real skin' effect. For a lighter coverage in summer, with added skincare benefits and SPF 30, I love Crème de la Mer Reparative Skintint.

Finish-wise, I find a hint of shine preferable to the deadening effect of too-matte foundation, or a heavy-handed application of powder. That said, a cloud of Caron Bulgarian-rose-scented loose powder applied with a goosedown puff is something everyone should delight in occasionally. Even the most ardent make-up minimalist seems to be fanatical about brows. I swear by MAC's Brow Set gel, while Polly Morgan (see page 30) is never fully groomed without her brow pencil.

I believe that the ritual of make-up is as much part of the feel-good moment as the end result. And that brings me to the grand finale – lips. Whether it's a minimal coat of balm (I recommend Clarins Extra-Firming Lip and Contour Balm or Lucas' Papaw Ointment), a sheer stain (Chanel Rouge Coco Shine), or a densely pigmented red straight from the bullet, it's nice to savour the moment.

For the ultimate red lip: **NARS, Shiseido, Topshop, Dior**

For elegant packaging: **Charlotte Tilbury, Tom Ford, Chanel** (above)

The Jeans

For something supposedly effortless and utilitarian, jeans sure take a lot of work to get right. But find the ones that work for you and you're sorted for life. Admittedly, jeans have been through the fashion wringer lately, meaning it's been almost impossible to find authentic, not-too-fashiony jeans that aren't 90 per cent Lycra, covered in pretend 'whiskers' or shredded to the 'nth' degree. So I recommend going back to basics and, luckily, Levi's is experiencing a renaissance. It has revived its 501s in a cut that's just boyfriend enough, and you can get the hems altered for free in its flagship stores. Also serving the Levi's loyalist is Re/Done, a Californian brand that finds vintage Levi's and tailors them for a lean (but not super-skinny) fit.

I like my denim clean and dark; it makes the jeans more versatile as they can be worn as easily with a suede cigarette pump as with a lace-up Oxford or Maison Margiela's Tabi boots. For these, I recommend Levi's Made & Crafted (its slightly more grown-up line), COS, Gap and M.i.H. Jeans. Perfumer Lyn Harris (see page 24) bulk-buys hers from A.P.C. (but you need patience to wear them in), while 6397 and Crippen are two newer brands whose denim is rooted in true blue perfection.

Worth a mention are the made-to-order jeans by Levi's Lot No. 1 and New York-based 3x1. These services involve choosing your cut, cloth, thread colour, buttons, and so on, from scratch and the process is tremendously fulfilling. Yes, it's expensive but choose wisely and these are an investment that should be worthwhile in the long run.

For boyish styling: **Levi's**, **A.P.C.** (above)

For dark denim: **3x1**, **6397**, **Crippen**

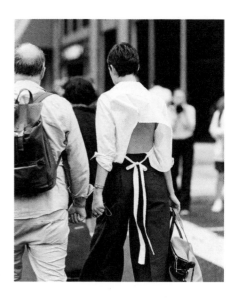

'It's all about the details. How many buttons do you want?
How long do you want the jacket? Where does it hit?'

CAROLINE ISSA

My favourite trick to de-formalize
a dressy shirt: push up the sleeves
and throw a sweater over the
shoulders.

Utilitarian style works best when paired with its opposite number. I love the unexpected playful punch of the orange eyewear with the muted khaki trench. It lifts the whole outfit, with not very much effort at all.

This gamine look is achieved with a sweet
collared shirt and a tucked-in sweater.
The belt is the understated-but-crucial
element that pulls everything together.

'I don't like to look masculine but I find boyish quite feminine and quite sexy.'

BELLA FREUD

A timeless, leather-strapped watch or minimalist jewellery are all that's needed to add refinement to an unbuttoned shirt.

The architectural cut of the jacket elevates these boyish, monochrome separates to a whole other level.

'The most important thing is to have comfort in your shoes. It's something very sensual.'

LAURENCE DACADE

Perfect pairing: mannish shoes benefit greatly from a slim cropped trouser, to draw the eye to the ankles.

Pyjama styling at its best in the casual guise of an oversized silk shirt, worn unbuttoned.

Who doesn't love a personal recommendation
from those 'in the know'? What follows
are the go-to brands and places that never
fail to delight, amuse and inform – from
neighbourhood cafés to consignment websites
to the best secret bookstore in London.

The Source Book

CHAPTER 4

Markets

Golborne Road Market,
London W10 5NR

Portobello's lesser-known
neighbour is Bella Freud's secret
source for vintage furniture and
Moroccan snacks. Fridays are
quieter but Saturdays more fun.

Sunbury Antiques Market,
Kempton Park Race Course,
Staines Road East, Sunbury-on-
Thames, Middlesex TW16 5AQ

sunburyantiques.com

Arrive at 7AM for the best pick
of French farmhouse furniture,
Belgian chandeliers and cheery
bric-a-brac from this popular
twice-monthly market.

Fort Greene Flea Market,
176 Lafayette Ave, Brooklyn,
NY 11238

brooklynflea.com

Set designer Jill Nicholls
recommends the Fort Greene
weekend flea market for
summer-Saturday foraging,
where she heads for the stall
selling classic French workwear.

Puces de Saint-Ouen, rue des
Rosiers, 93400 Saint-Ouen, Paris

Europe's most famous flea
market is Daphné Hézard's
weekend destination, where
everything from antique
furniture to military clothing
can be found.

Lifestyle Stores

Bella Freud, 49 Chiltern Street,
London W1U 6LX

bellafreud.com

Books, records, knitwear, perfume and candles – all can be found in Bella Freud's charming Chiltern Street shop, designed to feel like an extension of her cultured world.

The Conran Shop, Michelin House, 81 Fulham Road, London SW3 6RD

conranshop.co.uk

Interior nirvana for contemporary style geeks, selling classic furniture, vintage magazines and rustic kitchenware.

Liberty, Regent Street, London W1B 5AH

liberty.co.uk

Head here for beautiful textiles, unique fashion finds and the perfect teatime pit stop in British Arts and Crafts surroundings.

The New Craftsmen, 34 North Row, London W1K 6DG

thenewcraftsmen.com

This unique Mayfair concept store selling handmade homewares and crafts by new British artisans is a secret you'll want to keep to yourself.

Selfridges, 400 Oxford Street, London W1A 1AB

selfridges.com

London's one-stop shop for everything from Muji pens to an Apple upgrade. Its themed retail concepts and window displays attract legions of fans from around the globe.

The Shop at Bluebird, 350 King's Road, London SW3 5UU

theshopatbluebird.com

London's off-radar concept store that mixes iconic fashion-forward brands (J. W. Anderson, Comme des Garçons) with artisanal fragrances and an enviable library of coffee-table books.

Skandium, 86 Marylebone High Street, London W1U 4QS

skandium.com

Nothing bad could ever happen in this haven for all things Scandi and homely. Storage, glassware and children's books are a strong point.

Anthropologie, 50 Rockefeller Plaza, New York 10020

anthropologie.com

Head to 'Anthro' for gift shopping or just to be inspired by the breathtaking displays. Books, colourful ceramics and trinket trays are a big draw.

The Apartment, 76 Greene Street, New York 10012

theline.com

Founders Vanessa Traina and Morgan Wendelborn fill this by-appointment loft space with furniture, fashion, *objets* and photography finds, all available to buy. Think of it as like shopping in your most tasteful friend's impossibly chic apartment.

Dover Street Market, 160 Lexington Avenue, New York 10016

newyork.doverstreetmarket.com

Everybody's favourite high-low concept store. Whether you spend thousands on conceptual diamond jewellery or a few dollars on a pair of rustic socks, there's always a surprise to discover here.

Shinola, 177 Franklin Street, New York 10013

shinola.com

One for 'Made In America' enthusiasts, the New York flagship of this Detroit-based watches-and-leather-goods brand sells everything from beautiful unisex watches to vegetable-tanned leather accessories and even handmade bikes.

Astier de Villatte, 173 rue Saint-Honoré, 75001 Paris

astierdevillatte.com

Handmade ceramics and candles, plus a sideline in beautiful stationery, are the hallmarks of this most delightful of Parisian stores.

Florists

Tank, 91–93 Great Portland Street, London W1W 7NX

tankmagazine.com

For a last-minute gift, buy books and blooms from the front-of-house shop at Caroline Issa's *Tank* HQ.

Wild at Heart at Liberty, Great Marlborough Street, London W1B 5AH

wildatheart.com

Pick up fulsome peonies and English roses from Nikki Tibbles's Insta-famous outpost at the entrance of Liberty department store.

Chelsea Flower Market,
W 28th Street, New York 10001

This wholesale market is the first port of call for New York's interior decorators, set designers and flower enthusiasts. Get there before 10AM for the best picks.

Baltimore Bloemen,
Augustijnenstraat 35,
2000, Antwerp

baltimorebloemen.be

Famous for creating extravagant displays for Dior, florist Mark Colle exhibits the same taste for the offbeat but dramatic in his Antwerp flower shop.

Bookshops

Claire de Rouen, First Floor, 125 Charing Cross Road, London WC2H 0EW

clairederouenbooks.com

This hard-to-find store lets you linger as long as you like over its rare fashion 'zines' and collectible photo books.

Daunt Books, 83 Marylebone High Street, London W1U 4QW

dauntbooks.co.uk

An old-fashioned, English bookseller, Caroline Issa's local haunt specializes in maps and travel books in Edwardian, oak-panelled surroundings.

Idea Books, 101 Wardour Street, London W1F 0UG

idea-books.com

Specializing in fashion and photography, this by-appointment rare-books dealer is an Instagram sensation, followed by designers, creative directors and photographers.

Maison Assouline, 196a Piccadilly, London W1J 9EY

assouline.com

Situated in a magnificent former bank building designed by Edwin Lutyens, Prosper Assouline's London flagship is coffee-table-book heaven, with a beautiful in-house café too.

Dashwood Books, 33 Bond Street, New York 10012

dashwoodbooks.com

Head to Jill Nicholls's favourite photography bookshop to discover an esoteric edit of new and out-of-print books.

Strand Bookstore, 828 Broadway, New York 10003

strandbooks.com

Lose yourself for hours among the rare and used books in this cherished New York institution. The bohemian, anti-corporate vibe is a big draw.

Ofr, 20 rue Dupetit-Thouars, 75003 Paris

ofrsystem.com

Kris Kim's Paris buying trips are punctuated by an inspirational visit to Ofr for just-released art and design books and cult magazines.

Copyright, Nationalestraat 28a, 2000, Antwerp

copyrightbookshop.be

Designed by architect Vincent Van Duysen, this minimalist Antwerp bookshop is a blissful spot in which to explore the books on architecture, design and fashion.

Stationery

Smythson

smythson.com

You can't beat bespoke business cards and notecards from the Queen's stationer. Their blue-papered notebooks and diaries are the stuff of legend.

Kate Spade

katespade.co.uk

Kate Spade's upbeat, graphic-print notecards are perfect for when a rushed email just won't do.

McNally Jackson

mcnallyjacksonstore.com

Leather notebooks, Japanese writing implements, desks and lamps – get the whole kit and caboodle from this 'goods for the study' store.

Moleskine

moleskine.com

The notebooks of choice for eminent writers and designers – choose from original matte-black or colour-code with an array of primary brights.

Muji, 475 5th Avenue, New York 10017

muji.com

Nothing makes you feel more motivated than a blank Muji notebook and a potful of gel pens.

Rifle Paper Co.

riflepaperco.com

Beautifully illustrated and printed notecards that you'll want to keep for yourself.

Food Destinations

Charbonnel et Walker,
One The Royal Arcade, 28 Old
Bond Street, London W1S 4BT

charbonnel.co.uk

For special occasions, a sweet
treat from this heritage British
chocolatier, founded in 1875, is
always greatly appreciated. The
original New Bond Street store
still stands today.

La Fromagerie, 2–6 Moxon
Street, London, W1U 4EW

lafromagerie.co.uk

Marylebone's celebrated
cheese shop and café comes
recommended by perfumer
Lyn Harris. Order the brioche
toast for breakfast and then
take home a selection of its
renowned cheeses and cordials.

Leila's Shop, 15–17 Calvert
Avenue, London E2 7JP

Charming comfort food
served in a no-frills café with
a neighbourhood feel.

The Parlour,
Fortnum & Mason, 181
Piccadilly, London W1A 1ER

fortnumandmason.com

At this renowned ice-cream
parlour, a Piccadilly institution,
even your coffee comes served
with its own miniature ice-
cream cone.

Café Sabarsky, 1048 5th Ave,
New York 10028

Recommended by Kristen
Naiman, this Upper East Side
Viennese café serves pastries,
savoury treats and coffee to the
art lovers of the Neue Galerie.

Patisserie Burrow, 68 Jay Street,
119 Brooklyn, New York 11201

For something a little different,
Brooklyn's Patisserie Burrow is
known for its charming hand-
painted biscuits and animal-
shaped confectionery.

Café de Flore, 172 Boulevard
Saint-Germain, 75006 Paris

The preferred hangout of every
chic Parisian artist and thinker
who ever lived, including
Jean Cocteau. Sophie Hersan
enjoyed coffee and eggs here
with the late, great Chloé
founder, Gaby Aghion.

Rose Bakery, 30 rue
Debelleyme, 75003 Paris

Delicious savoury tarts and
cakes accompanied by organic
teas and juices.

Beauty Stores

Aēsop

Aesop.com

The familiar amber bottles and hand creams are a major fixture in the gentlewoman's bathroom. And why not, when these tubes and apothecary bottles are full of such plant-based goodness?

Perfumer H, 106a Crawford Street, London W1H 2HZ

perfumerh.com

This concept store and working laboratory by Lyn Harris sells seasonal perfumes and candles in handblown glass vessels. Try the bespoke service to create your own signature scent.

Editions de Parfums, 94 Greenwich Avenue, New York 10011

Frédéric Malle's West Village perfume store celebrates architecture and scent in a unique setting designed by Steven Holl. A must-visit for fragrance lovers. I recommend the Dries Van Noten perfume.

Buly 1803, 6 rue Bonaparte, 75006 Paris

buly1803.com

This, the favourite destination of Caroline Issa and Sophie Hersan, specializes in water-based perfumes and all-natural beauty potions. Do linger and soak up the décor and intimate atmosphere.

Caron, 90 rue du Faubourg Saint-Honoré, 75008 Paris

parfumscaron.com

Step back in time to an era of feathery powder puffs and old-school perfume flacons in Caron's genteel Paris store.

Santa Maria Novella

santamarianovellausa.com

There's something extremely seductive about the creams, soaps and colognes, handmade in Florence, inside these gorgeously packaged bottles and pots.

Museums

Sir John Soane's Museum, 13 Lincoln's Inn Fields, London WC2A 3BP

soane.org

Immerse yourself in the work of neo-classical architect Sir John Soane, whose former home has been preserved for public viewing.

Tate Modern, Bankside, London SE1 9TG

tate.org.uk

A must-visit for blockbuster exhibitions with one of the best permanent art collections in the world.

Victoria & Albert Museum,
Cromwell Road, London
SW7 2RL

vam.ac.uk

There's usually a great fashion extravaganza to be seen here, and the late-night events are always enlightening and entertaining.

Brooklyn Museum,
200 Eastern Parkway,
New York 11238

brooklynmuseum.org

For a less touristy experience, the Brooklyn Museum has an impressive programme of contemporary art and photography exhibitions. Make time for a stroll in the neighbouring Brooklyn Botanic Garden.

Fondation Louis Vuitton,
8 avenue du Mahatma Gandhi, Bois de Boulogne, 75116 Paris

fondationlouisvuitton.fr

Lose yourself for hours in this Frank Gehry-designed modern-art museum.

Parks

Holland Park, Ilchester Place, London W8

Head for the Japanese Kyoto Garden for a moment of quiet contemplation.

Jardin du Luxembourg,
rue de Médicis – rue de Vaugirard, 75006 Paris

Enjoy Paris at its poetic best with a stroll through this romantic park.

Jardin des Plantes,
57 rue Cuvier, 75005 Paris

This picturesque botanical garden is Daphné Hézard's chosen spot for a morning jog.

Places to Stay

Claridge's, Brook Street, London W1K 4HR

claridges.co.uk

If money is no object, spend at least one night at Claridge's and enjoy a quintessentially English afternoon tea while you're there.

Airbnb

airbnb.com

Adventurous globetrotters may prefer the Airbnb approach for a more live-like-a-local travel experience.

The Bowery Hotel, 335 Bowery, New York 10003

theboweryhotel.com

For the ultimate combination of homely comfort with upscale service, the Bowery is an unbeatable choice for a long city break in a vibrant location.

3 Rooms, 5 rue de Moussy, 75004 Paris

Modernist fetishists will love these three apartment suites, owned and furnished by Azzedine Alaïa, with classic design pieces from Jean Prouvé, Charlotte Perriand and Arne Jacobsen.

Boulevard Leopold Bed and Breakfast, Belgiëlei 135, 2018 Antwerp

boulevard-leopold.be

Less a hotel, more a feeling of staying at a beautiful private residence. This posh B&B in Antwerp's Jewish quarter is an atmospheric and homely gem.

Soho House Berlin, Torstraße 1, 10119 Berlin

sohohouseberlin.com

The kind of home-away-from-home you expect from a Soho House hotel, with the added bonus of The Store, an outpost of Alex Eagle's delightful concept store.

E-tailers

1stdibs.com

Scroll through rare antique furniture, obscure couture and iconic jewels from the best independent dealers across the globe.

everlane.com

For the thoughtful, style-conscious consumer, Everlane keeps prices and waste down by eschewing the fast fashion approach and only selling online. A secret source for boyish basics.

farfetch.com

This online marketplace lets you shop from independent designer boutiques around the world, including Browns in London and The Webster in Miami.

lagarconne.com

E-tail heaven for grown-up tomboys, selling Acne Studios, Sacai and Maison Margiela alongside its in-house line, La Garçonne Moderne.

lyst.com

For the time-crunched shopper, Lyst aggregates the best e-tailers into one easy-to-shop edit. Streamline your feed according to the brands and stores you like.

manufactum.co.uk

If beechwood letter trays and handmade glycerine soap turn you on, you'll love the excellent edit of lifestyle goods from this cult German lifestyle site.

vestiairecollective.com

Where fashion-industry insiders offload last season's Isabel Marant, A.P.C. and Comme des Garçons. It's all verified and authenticated but be quick – the best pieces go instantly.

High-street Stores

COS

cosstores.com

The thinking woman's high-street store. Stand-out items include coats, knitwear and jewellery, plus there's a brilliant in-house magazine too.

Gap

gap.com

Still a great go-to for basics. Head here for white shirts, cashmere knits and indigo 'sexy boyfriend' jeans, which they'll alter while you wait.

J.Crew

jcrew.com

Bypass the statement fashion items in lieu of the classics. J.Crew excels at menswear-inspired blazers and trousers, as well as the best pointy heels. Don't forget the men's and kids' department for hidden gems.

Jigsaw

jigsaw.com

Recently revamped, Jigsaw's efforts to use British manufacturing for many of its knits and coats are laudable. The men's tailoring also deserves a special mention.

& Other Stories

stories.com

An excellent all-rounder, with a fantastic beauty section where you can browse at your leisure.

Uniqlo

uniqlo.com

The best thing about Uniqlo (apart from its men's shirts), is its designer collaborations by Christophe Lemaire and Inès de la Fressange.

Whistles

whistles.com

Fashion meets function with an accessibly priced line in leather jackets, cool coats and non-corporate workwear.

Denim

3x1

3x1.us

Indulge in the brilliant bespoke service, where you can choose the fit, denim, thread colour and details.

Crippen

crippen-la.com

The go-to jeans if you love grown-up denim in a slim-but-not-skinny cut.

Levi's

levi.com

You can't beat 501 jeans, whether that's white for summer or true blue. Get complimentary alterations in the flagship stores.

M.i.H. Jeans

mih-jeans.com

Try the bestselling Phoebe boyfriend jeans and the shirts and knits to go with them.

Vetements

vetementswebsite.com

Deconstructed jeans, re-tailored from old lived-in Levi's, courtesy of a design team that originates from Maison Margiela.

Specialist Fashion

Bicester Village, 50 Pingle Drive, Bicester OX26 6WD

bicestervillage.com

Located in Oxfordshire, England, this is the best outlet village in Europe. Put Céline, Saint Laurent, Prada and Smythson at the top of your list.

Church's

church-footwear.com

Famous for its boyish brogues and Derbys in plain glossy leather or decorated with studs.

Egg, 36 Kinnerton Street, London SW1X 8ES

eggtrading.com

Maureen Doherty's off-the-radar store is a blissful retail treasure trove. Buy a perfect white shirt or just come and gaze at the beauty of it all.

Hostem, 41–43 Redchurch Street, London E2 7DJ

hostem.co.uk

This East London boutique champions the finest in contemporary fashion artisanship, including Toogood, CristaSeya, Dries Van Noten and Yang Li – all beautifully displayed.

Niketown

nike.com

For basic sports kit in an inspiring environment, you can't beat Niketown. Nike Air Max and untampered-with grey marl jogging bottoms get my vote.

A.P.C.

apc.fr

Known for its boy–girl elevated basics. Pick up a cult candle, classic mac or some iconic denim. The Butler programme sells pre-loved A.P.C. jeans, as bought by Sophie Hersan.

Charvet, 28 Place Vendôme, 75001 Paris

The ultimate in luxury shirting. Go to the Paris store for the made-to-measure experience and order some monogrammed pyjamas while you're there.

LaContrie, 11 rue de la Sourdière, 75001 Paris

lacontrie.com

The ultimate bespoke handbag experience; mix and match the style, leather, pockets, zips, handles and colour of stitching from a range of beautifully designed components.

Olatz

olatz.com

Olatz Schnabel's classic silk pyjamas come in the simplest of cuts but the most dizzying array of colours. Each pair takes two weeks to make but the result is worth the wait.

Luxury Brands

Acne Studios

acnestudios.com

Luxurious tomboy staples, with a sideline in book publishing and an excellent bi-annual magazine.

Céline

celine.com

Ultra-minimalist overcoats, suits and trousers from a brand that knows how to design for women.

Dries Van Noten

driesvannoten.be

When you want to inject some colour, print and romance into your wardrobe, head to Dries.

Hermès

hermes.com

For lovers of slow fashion, everything from the leather-bound notebooks to the enamel bangles telegraphs its buy-now-use-forever ethos.

Margaret Howell

margarethowell.co.uk

Thoroughly sensible yet always stylish, with a focus on traditional menswear fabrics and a dedication to British manufacturing. The MHL line is the excellent diffusion line.

Ralph Lauren

ralphlauren.com

The very embodiment of the word 'lifestyle'; splash out on the camel coats and men's cashmeres, or settle for the Jamaica scented candle.

The Row, 8440 Melrose Place, Los Angeles, CA 90069

therow.com

Grown-up, stealth-luxe pieces worth saving for, the Melrose Place store is styled like a house you want to move into.

Jewellery and Watches

Cartier

cartier.co.uk

From the understated Love bangle to the dramatic Panthère jewellery, these timeless baubles are worth investing in.

Dinh Van

dinhvan.com

Everyday jewellery that's refined and adaptable.

Jaeger-LeCoultre

jaeger-lecoultre.com

Opt for the understated Reverso watch, a design classic originally created for energetic polo players.

Le Gramme

legramme.com

Super-slimline men's bracelets, loved by women. Each bangle is made from recycled sterling silver or red gold and named after its gram weight.

Repossi, Place Vendôme, 75001 Paris

repossi.com

The heritage, fine-jewellery maker is now creatively helmed by the elegant Gaia Repossi, who has modernized the house with her cool, minimalist flair.

Swatch

swatch.com

Affordable, utilitarian, but loads of fun; hunt out vintage ones for the best graphics.

Menswear Stores

Mr Porter

mrporter.com

The menswear outpost of Net-a-Porter has surprising finds that would suit women equally well. Leather-goods (I love Valextra) come in great colours and are often a simpler design and better priced.

Paul Smith, 9 Albemarle Street, London W1S 4HH

paulsmith.co.uk

The best selection of rainbow-hued cashmere, if you like your knits oversized. This store also sells beautifully selected art.

The Real McCoy's, 10 Greene Street, New York 10013

realmccoysnyc.com

American-style military and utility classics lovingly reproduced in Japan. The outerwear (pea coats, bomber jackets and raincoats) is especially strong.

RRL, 16 Mount Street, London W1K 2RH

ralphlauren.com

Ralph Lauren's worn-in shabby chic menswear line looks just as good on women (if not better).

Antiques and Vintage

Alfie's Antiques, 13–25 Church Street, London NW8 8DT

alfiesantiques.com

Caroline Issa's favourite London hunting ground for twentieth-century furniture, homewares and a little fashion. Mull over your purchases in the café upstairs.

Byronesque

byronesque.com

This e-commerce destination specializes in the cultest of vintage fashion from the likes of Comme des Garçons, Helmut Lang and Maison Margiela and will track down special requests.

Cassie Mercantile, 14 Addison Avenue, London W11 4QR

cassiemercantile.com

A well-regarded treasure trove of utilitarian menswear, eclectic textiles and other inspirational finds displayed just so in Graham Cassie's Holland Park hideaway. By appointment.

Decades Inc, 8214 Melrose Ave, Los Angeles, CA 90046

decadesinc.com

Get a history lesson with your original YSL Le Smoking from the best vintage detectives in the business.

Paula Rubenstein, 21 Bond Street, New York 10012

paularubenstein.com

Books, mirrors, textiles and glassware, you name it, Paula has it haphazardly arranged in her rummage-friendly antique store.

Utilitarian Style

ESK Cashmere

eskcashmere.com

Rustic Scottish knitwear in cashmere or Shetland wool comes in classic, unisex shapes. For the ultimate personalization, choose a made-to-order knit in one of 100 colours to be made especially for you.

Labour and Wait, 85 Redchurch Street, London E2 7DJ

labourandwait.co.uk

Buying the most mundane items feels exciting in this charming green-tiled emporium of enamel plates, sensible fishermen's knits and gardening tools.

Native & Co, 116 Kensington Park Road, London W11 2PW

nativeandco.com

A stone's throw from Portobello Market, this tranquil boutique is devoted to no-fuss Japanese and Taiwanese design. Canvas totes, earthenware jugs and fine-grained maple furniture will lure you in.

Tiina the Store, 216 Main Street, Amagansett, NY 11930

tiinathestore.com

The ultimate in everyday utility-luxe, the shapes are utilitarian but the feel is far from soulless. Find handknit sweaters and Feit sneakers alongside indigo-dyed kimonos and mohair blankets in Tiina Laakkonen's cult Amagansett store.

Cinemas

Electric Cinema, 191 Portobello Road, London W11 2ED

electriccinema.co.uk

The kind of plush cinema where you can snuggle under a blanket and have gourmet burgers brought to your seat. Splash out for date night, and book early.

Film Forum, 209 W Houston Street, New York, NY 10014

filmforum.org

Kick back and relax in Sophie Auster's favourite downtown indie cinema, where foreign and art-house films have been shown since the 1970s.

Secret Cinema

secretcinema.org

Taking cinema-going to a whole other level, this is a fun, themed experience for adventurous film buffs.

Index

Picture Credits / Acknowledgments

All photography on pages 16, 42–47, 54–59, 90–101 © Max Dworkin, www.maxdworkin.com. All photography on pages 18–41, 48–53, 60–65 © Kasia Bobula, www.kasiabobula.com. All photography on pages 66–89, 102 © Elise Toïdé, www.elisetoide.com.

Page 8 Portrait of Gabrielle Chanel and her dog Gigot at her villa La Pausa in the South of France, near Roquebrune. Copyright: All Rights Reserved/Chanel Collection; page 11 top left © Bettmann/Corbis; page 11 top right Henry Clarke © Condé Nast Archive/Corbis; page 11 bottom © John Springer Collection/Corbis; page 12 top courtesy Jacques Barsac; page 12 bottom left Getty (photo by Ron Galella/WireImage); page 12 bottom right Theodore Miller © courtesy Lee Miller Archives, England 2016. All rights reserved; page 15 top © Alain Dejean/Sygma/Corbis; page 15 bottom left photo by Jean-Jacques Bernier/Gamma-Rapho via Getty Images; page 15 bottom right © Andrew Goetz/Corbis; page 23 top courtesy Gladys Perint Palmer, originally created for The Telegraph; page 33 artwork courtesy Celia Hempton and Southard Reid, London; page 65 top artwork by David Bromley; page 77 top drawing by Jean-Louis Dumas; page 93 bottom right illustration by Tim Burton; page 94 artwork by Jon Kessler; page 104 Filippa K, AW15, Florence Coat; page 105 Joseph Tuxedo Wool Joel Trousers, www.joseph-fashion.com; page 106 &Daughter/

and-daughter.com; page 107 180 Loafer copyright J.M. Weston; page 108 features of the Shinola Runwell include Super-LumiNova printed dial details and a solid stainless-steel case; page 109 Paul Smith Ltd; page 110 Bally B Turn Bag in Caper Green Calf Leather; page 111 courtesy Helmut Lang; page 112 courtesy equipment.fr; page 113 Burberry at matchesfashion.com; page 114 Mesh Triangle Bra by Land of Women; page 115 courtesy Charlotte Olympia; page 116 Karen Walker Eyewear; page 117 Dinh Van Menottes necklace in yellow gold; page 118 jcrew.com; page 119 Acqua di Colonia Melograno by Officina Profumo Farmaceutica di Santa Maria Novella, Florence, Italy; page 120 TS Brando by agnès b; page 121 courtesy Brooks Brothers; page 112 Margaret Howell Navy Silk Twill Grid Spot Scarf; page 123 Common Projects Original Achilles Low. Photo courtesy Common Projects; page 124 Smythson Grosvenor bijou organizer in red; page 125 courtesy Vinaya; page 126 Aesop Hand Balm, www.aesop.com; page 127 Chanel Rouge Coco in Gabrielle; page 128 APC Petit Standard Men's Jeans, www.apc.fr.

All photographs on pages 129–139 by Vanessa Jackman. Reasonable attempts were made to contact the people photographed and the publisher would be pleased to correct any omissions in future editions of this book. Page 130 top left Caroline Issa;

page 130 bottom right Tamu McPherson; page 131 top left Ashley Owens; page 131 top right Rebecca Laurey; page 134 left Natalia Alaverdian; page 134 bottom right Miroslava Duma; page 135 top left Sabrina Meijer; page 136 Elizabeth von Gutmann; page 138 bottom left Jenny Walton; page 138 top right Kamilya Kuspan; page 139 bottom right Yasmin Sewell.

Illustrations on pages 142–157 by Masumi Briozzo.

My biggest and most heartfelt thanks go to the fantastic women who agreed to be interviewed and photographed for this book. Thank you for your time, commitment and wonderful insights. To the PRs, PAs and managers, thanks for believing in the project and giving me access to jam-packed schedules.

I'm extremely proud of the imagery in this book, so a huge thank you goes to our dream team of photographers – Kasia Bobula, Max Dworkin, Elise Toïdé and Vanessa Jackman. I'm forever grateful for your enthusiasm and dedication. Thank you also to Lucy Maria for your tenacity and attention to detail, and to Masumi Briozzo for translating my vague design references into something elegant and beautiful.

To the team at Laurence King, thank you for taking a leap of faith. Thank you to Helen Rochester for

early encouragement and to my editor Clare Double for extreme patience and teaching me that there is always a solution.

For idea-bouncing and support, I'm grateful to Virginie Vaulot, Dal Chodha, Talib Choudhry, David Watts, Julia Williams, Alex Shah, Circe Hamilton, Alice King, Susan Wylie, Wendy Brandes, Preston Davis, Jason Waterworth and Lisa Patten.

For ongoing cheerleading and allowing me to vent during times of mercury retrograde, thank you Alison Bishop, Alyson Walsh, Roddy Frame, Rachel Bishop, Emma Miranda Moore, Simon Glazin, Grahame Martin and the Cosmeal clan.

For inspiration and pushing me out of my comfort zone, I'd like to thank my early mentors Caroline Baker, Kay McMahon, Bruce Webster and Celia Duncan. And thank you Penny Martin and all the gentlewomen out there whose influence helped crystallize the vision for this book.

The opportunity to write this book would not have come about had I not started on my blogging adventure in 2007. To all those who have played a part in Disneyrollergirl, thank you for reading, commenting and encouraging me and so many others to use our voices.

To my favourite gentlewomen and gentleman, mum, Roxanna and David, thank you for everything.